PHOENIX STYLE

Stories to Ignite Your Entrepreneurial Spirit

Rachael Ansar
Melissa Kirkpatrick
Arielle Schmidt
Kimberlee Vollbrecht

Angel Hicks
Jaime Lyons
Alex Toth

Influence **Network** *Media*

Copyright @ 2022 Influence Network Media

All Rights Reserved. Apart from any fair dealing for purposes of research or private study, or criticism or review, as permitted under the Copyright, Designs and Patents Act 1988, this publication may only be reproduced, stored or transmitted, in any form or by any means, with the prior permission in writing of the copyright owner, or in the case of the reprographic reproduction in accordance with the terms of licenses issued by the Copyright Licensing Agency. Enquires concerning reproduction outside those terms should be sent to the publisher.

Contents

	Foreword	v
	Introduction	1
1.	The Ember That Wouldn't Go Out	3
	Arielle Schmidt	15
2.	Energize Productivity and Put Distraction to Sleep!	17
	Rachael Ansar	39
3.	The Evolution of a Networking Introvert	41
	Angel Hicks	59
4.	You are the Creator of Your Success	61
	Melissa Kirkpatrick	77
5.	Better Business	81
	Alex Toth	93
6.	Aspire to Inspire	95
	Jaime Lyons	109
7.	Reluctant Entrepreneur	111
	Kim Vollbrecht	123
	Conclusion	125
	About the Publisher	127

Women in Business Book Series 129

Book Smarts Business Podcast 131

Foreword

April Hurst | Entrepreneur, Author, Keynote Speaker, Online Marketing & Certified Life Coach.

Women. In a nutshell, WE. ARE. POWER. After all, we have the ability to birth a human. Not only is that beyond mind blowing, but it is a testament to how the women in Phoenix Style have discovered their authentic power to live a life of genuine meaning and purpose.

There are two ways to live one's life: as a sheep or as a rhinoceros.

Sheep follow the crowd. They're afraid to break away from the pack or embark into unknown territory. They move in packs. They prefer to take direction from others.

Rhinos, however, feel called to the jungle; but guess what also lies in wait out there? Lions, tigers, and creepy crawly things that only come out at night. There is a massive amount of uncertainty within the jungle. There is often no known road to take. You have to forge your path and, in some cases, take out your machete and cut your way through the thickest brush to get to a clearing where you can see.

This is often when and where we throw in the towel; because

it just gets too hard. Your arms are tired and the sweltering heat from the sun becomes almost unbearable. The key word here is almost.

Applying this metaphor to modern life…

As you cut your way through the rejection, naysayers, and self doubt, you see a summit far off in the distance. There is a motherland where you know your dreams are a reality. You always knew it was there. There was something in your heart, deep in your soul, that told you that there was more out there. The discomfort along the way was a means to a more meaningful life. That doesn't mean creepy crawlies disappear and there won't be a tiger that will jump out periodically from behind a tree; but it does mean you have a new vision for your business, for your family, and for yourself.

Regardless of what challenges arise, you do see the summit.

When things don't seem to be coming together quite as you thought they would, the summit is always there.

That summit becomes your lifeline. It is the way. The truth that you've held in your being from the moment you knew you were born; you were designed to do more, become more, and live fully and wholly.

The women whose words you will read in Phoenix Style have all had their fair share of trials, tribulations, and windy roads along their path to success. They began a journey of a thousand miles before they could clearly see their summit. Are you willing to start your race without knowing exactly where the finish line is? Can you, or will you, start down a new path when the summit can not even be seen with the naked eye? Most importantly, can you live a life of authenticity and inspire others even before you've made it to the top?

Everyone wants to see the revelation, but these women who are involved in and contributed to Phoenix Style share their genesis along with many other impactful books.

If you are willing to do the same, then you'll find yourself amongst a rare breed of humans who stumbled through the jungle, stayed focused on the horizon, reinvented themselves like the Phoenix, and landed atop their summit.

Introduction

After graduating from college, we wished there was a manual or playbook for women to guide us on our path to success in life and career. And with each milestone, from career progression, to becoming a mom, as we left the corporate world, and again when we started businesses as entrepreneurs – we have wished for another *magical* manual or playbook.

Of course, we knew *magic* wasn't the answer. Yet an enduring power continued to surface among our tribe. We started Influence Network Media to help business experts find their voice to become authors and influencers. And the swell of women that came forward was inspiring.

When talking with potential authors, many women spoke of their desire for guidance from other strong female leaders to understand their journey to success.

Moms came forward who wanted to tell stories of how becoming a mom made them a better leader. Entrepreneurs wanted to share their experience and provide guidance to the future entrepreneurs. Women in male-dominated industries wanted to show how our gender when fully embraced can be quite a superpower, not a weakness. And men and women wanting to share their knowledge and expertise to champion women leaders and create a more inclusive world.

These conversations are the reason we created the Women in Business Book Series. This is our gift to women (today and future generations) to guide them toward success in life, in their career and in business. Twenty-five authors have provided their stories, insights, and guidance to help women shine both professionally and personally. Our message is uplifting. It's heart-driven. It's breaking through barriers.

Our book series summary says it all:

> "In this series you will explore the stories, guidance, and dedication of truly dedicated and hardworking women who excel in their fields – not despite the fact that they're women, but because they are women."

Use these books as guides. Gift these books to the women in your life. Connect with the authors and share your story. Our society and the next generation of female leaders are watching us very closely. And with that comes great responsibility. Our world will be a better and more inclusive place, with the kinds of connection, learning moments, and critical conversation ignited with this series.

We welcome you to join the conversation.

~Jodi Brandstetter and Melanie Booher, Co-founders of Influence Network Media

I.

The Ember That Wouldn't Go Out

Arielle Schmidt | Owner at Tranquility Rising

I believe that there are many paths in life that can bring contentment, but for some, contentment isn't enough; there's an ember that burns and it just needs nurturing to be re-sparked. That is exactly my story: a story of how I reignited my spark in India and how I transitioned from being a corrections officer to becoming a holistic practitioner of Thai Yoga Therapy and owner of my own business, Tranquility Rising.

As I look back at my story, there are many moments in time that had to happen for me to find my way to and on this journey, and to discover the courage to say "yes" when those moments came forward. In college I signed up for a semester of Pilates for an easy GPA booster, but the first day I arrived I was told the semester would be yoga instead. I was disgruntled with the news as I thought yoga was a joke, and I also didn't know much about yoga since there weren't any studios where I grew up in South Dakota. But it was an easy A, so I rolled my eyes, rolled out my mat, and showed up for every class. As the semester continued, my perspective of yoga shifted. It allowed me to tap into this part of myself that I didn't even know was there; a place that was calm and content, and it really helped me combat the stress of college and my part-time job as a corrections officer. By the end of the semester I told myself, "I am going to go to India and study this. I don't know when or how, but I'm going to go." Little did I know that that seemingly random statement would come to fruition six years later. For now it would slip into the archives of my mind, patiently waiting to be reignited.

After college I moved from South Dakota to Cincinnati, Ohio, where I found myself working full-time as a corrections officer starting in February of 2014. The pay was high and the overtime was abundant. I was good at my job, I was a Field Training Officer for new hires, running the trustee worker program, and setting myself up for a promotion within the jail. Things were great – except I was working anywhere between 60-80 hours a week and slowly getting very burned out; with both physical and emotional fatigue. As a female corrections officer working in a county jail, I found myself slowly numbing out to cope with constant fight-or-flight situations, and I was learning to show no emotions when inmates would lob the vilest insults and threats at me. I knew that if I showed emotion, they'd know exactly how to get under my skin for my eight to sixteen hour shift with them. This is what led me back to yoga. I knew I needed a way to reconnect to myself, allow myself to feel those emotions that were bottled up, and reset my nervous system. So, I found myself showing up for a Yin Yoga class at the Cincinnati Yoga School in August of 2016. The first thing out of the instructor's mouth was, "Don't forget, we're headed to India in January for our 200 hour yoga teacher training." I looked up from my mat in total disbelief of what I had just heard. I asked myself, "Did I just hear that right? India for a month? Yes, I did." The teacher training would run from mid-January 2017 to mid-February of 2017. Due to the extreme amount of overtime at the jail, I didn't even know if I could get thirty days off in a row. I had the time to take off as I had used minimal amounts of my vacation time since I was hired, and I knew I had to take the risk. The next day I emptied the little I had in my savings account, went back to the yoga school, and handed over a check for $3,000 knowing that I might not be able to go and could lose that money.

However, as though the universe was on my side, the majority of my time off was approved and there was miraculously enough staffing for the period I had requested off. Next thing I knew it was January 2017 and I was on a flight to India. I was nervous, sick to my stomach, and beyond scared. "What if I didn't like the training? What if I got sick? Why did I say yes to this?" When I arrived in India, the corrections officer inside of me kept me guarded and removed from interacting in the group, allowing me to be an observer instead of a participant. I showed up to class daily and just listened, soaking up what was taught. By day three, I was already counting down the days until my return, and I was annoyed that we were going to learn Thai Yoga Massage. I didn't want to learn massage; I didn't want to touch people; I just wanted to learn yoga. I kept looking at our itinerary to see when we'd get back to the postures of yoga – but the deeper we went into studying the meridian lines and the connections that the physical aches and pains have to our emotional states, something inside me clicked. That ember had been sparked. I was now curious as to what my body was saying, and I felt so drawn towards diving in deeper.

At the end of day five, I wrote in my travel journal about how my lifestyle had become toxic to my system and how my job as a corrections officer was just adding to the fire of my imbalance. Imagine trying to ignite a fire and continuing to blow on that fire; not only does it start but it also gets bigger and bigger with the more oxygen added to it, creating a potential out of control fire. Based on the elemental practice of working with the five great elements (Earth, Water, Fire, Air, and Space) and knowing how they interact with each other, excess fire leads to a domineering, aggressive, hyperactive, and competitive personality. This wasn't a negative aspect for my job as a corrections officer, but it was hurting me in my personal life as I didn't know how to shut that down except to numb out and become a zombie. It was no longer healthy or sustainable.

India had many ups and downs for me. It pushed me out of my comfort zone, and it made me take a really personal look at who I was and ultimately what I wanted out of my life. I knew I didn't want to keep up the sixty-eighty-hour a week workload, nor did I feel like being threatened with sexual assault, verbal insults, potential body fluids, or dealing with a deregulated nervous system from the hyperawareness my body was always in. The last day I was in India I wrote, "Is this truly what I envision for my life? I enjoy being in charge of what I do. I don't really want to retire from the jail even though it allows freedom, money, vacation, and personal stability. But what if I can make this (Thai Yoga) successful? Can I not have the same result?" I knew in those last days I had to create a plan to do more training, because if I returned to the jail without a plan then the ember that was sparked here in India would go out for good.

I returned from India and on my first day back, I was forced to work a sixteen-hour shift. It was abundantly clear that I was right: I needed to do something; and soon. So, I went home and immediately signed up for a two week Thai Yoga training in Costa Rica for August of 2017. As I pursued this vision of what I wanted to do, I always seemed to experience sadness and anxiety. The sadness was due to not having a lot of people in my corner rooting for me as well as walking away from my second family at the jail. We all worked so many hours together, and we trusted each other to have one another's backs, but I knew that ultimately once I removed myself from the position, most of the relationships would end. The anxiety stemmed from the possibility of failing. I have always strived to be the best regardless of what I was doing, and I can be a harsh critic of myself. The endless questioning from family and friends made me feel I had to prove I wasn't making a colossal mistake. But a friend told me, "You're exactly where you're supposed to be. If you weren't meant to be there, life would've taken you somewhere else. Life is good like that."

While I was in Costa Rica I had a one-on-one with the instructor who sat me down and asked me why I couldn't go back and quit my job. Overwhelming fear surfaced for me; to uproot my financial security without a plan was absolute insanity. I had a two-year plan to leave the jail. She responded in shock, "Two years?!? What would you do if your dream wasn't two years away but only six weeks?" Again, sheer panic emerged at the thought of walking away from financial security. "What would I do if I failed to thrive? Do I want to hustle and struggle for who knows how long?" When I returned from that training, I took a hard look at my life and my relationships and knew right then and there, "Okay, I guess I'm in!" The overtime was getting worse at the jail and it was no longer mostly voluntary, but forced. Plus, female officer shortages were causing us to lose even our days off because two females had to be on shift at all times. How much more was I willing to give up in and from my life? How much longer would I put up with the promise of "we're hiring more people" just for them to quit because of the burnout before even a year hits? I returned from Costa Rica at the end of August 2017, and in September of 2017 I created my LLC, Tranquility Rising.

At this point, I started to search for ways to gain clients. On my days off from the jail, I would schedule networking meetings with yoga studios and holistic health practitioners, and I signed up for many vendor events to showcase what Thai Yoga is. I also started to see clients in my home, which was something I did not want to do, because I didn't want my address to be out there for ex-inmates to find me. So, I set out to find office space that I could afford. I came across an office space that was so small, but it was $300 a month, and I knew it was now or never. I had to jump and trust myself or let the dream die.

October of 2017 is when I moved into that office space. I didn't know how I was going to have time to see clients with my schedule at the jail, but I wasn't about to let this dream escape me; no matter how tired I was. I remember having a client scheduled for 6:00 a.m., but I was forced into overtime at the jail and didn't get off until 4:00 a.m. So, I slept in the studio, saw my client, went home to sleep, and then returned to the jail for overtime at noon to work a 12 hour shift. Again, as the overtime mounted, I realized I was going to have to make the scariest decision of my life: walk away from a job that had financial stability, benefits, and retirement. I knew I had to make it five years to take my retirement with me, so in February 2018 when I had made it five years to the date, I put my two weeks' notice in. I bawled my eyes out as I turned in my uniform. It had been a part of my identity for so long, and the crushing fear of "Am I making the right choice?" flashed through my mind with overwhelming self-doubt.

The first six months of self-employment were rough. I was setting up at vendor events two or three times a month, networking every single day when I didn't have a client, and sometimes meeting over ten different practitioners in a week. I was on a mission to understand clients on a deeper level, and through connecting with practitioners who were approaching health in a non-Western way, it intrigued me to learn even more. I knew I wanted to bring more depth to what I was bringing to the community; depth that surpassed the traditional view of Thai Yoga Massage. So, I stuck to refusing to advertise as solely "massage" and continued to focus on the emotional pain people had locked away in the tissues of their bodies. I learned that our issues are rooted in the tissues, and there's no way around that except to bring awareness to those deep-rooted issues, so we can start to shift the ways we interact in all aspects of our life.

When I was searching out vendor spaces, I knew I had to have space to demonstrate what I did. I was adamant about educating my potential clients to look beyond the traditional aspect of Thai Yoga Massage and see clearly that it's much more than a massage, and that massage is just a safe doorway into this work that helps people open up, connect, and tune back into themselves. I'd have potential clients tell me where they were hurting, and then I'd give a quick ten-minute demonstration. While I was working on them, I'd start going through some of the emotional ties that that area of the body holds. Almost every single person was shocked. They couldn't believe I could pinpoint the issues they were experiencing in their life based solely on a physical touch.

When I'd meet with practitioners one-on-one, my goal was not to see what I could get from them in terms of referrals; instead I looked for practitioners whom I would genuinely love the possibility of working with. One perk was being able to offer a mini session to these practitioners to really show them what my practice was about. My philosophy of offering the mini sessions was to allow them to understand me as a practitioner. They could ask me about my story, and I was able to share my expertise of what they might need to work on and plant the seed for them to think of me if they ran into a block with one of their clients. These meetings were also great practice to deepen my skills as a bodyworker. For me just starting out, it was a win-win: I was able to meet with people I had great respect for and practice my skills at the same time.

Allowing practitioners and potential clients to see my authenticity of having their best interest at heart is what drove me to network so passionately. If someone came to me and I wasn't the right fit, I wanted to have recommendations of who would be. I learned that my goal when I work with clients is for them to lean into their own intuition to know what's best for their journey. This means I take a complete natural approach to sales; clients never feel pressure to say yes to working with me. The only thing I ask of them is to be radically honest with themselves and with me if they want to work with me or not. It frees the energy between us and makes clear the next path on their journey. So many entrepreneurs are so desperate to make the sale that they lose the fact that they can't help with everything, and they cannot help everyone. So, I make it my mission to know my limits, and to be honored when I've been part of someone's journey even if it was just to point them in a better direction.

I did have to supplement my income by teaching yoga during these first six months. While some consider having to find supplemental income as a failure, I looked at it as a way to network through a new avenue. But on the other hand, I hated teaching a power yoga class at 6:00 a.m. I hated working for someone else and being told how to interact with people and how to teach. For some reason it felt more restrictive than being at the jail. I look back now and realize how that was the fire within me screaming to trust myself. "You're on the right path; this is a temporary moment so you can continue to grow!" During this time, I chose to keep training and I did take on financial strains to keep pursuing training and coaching. I was thirsty to deepen my knowledge of what clients might need, and to be truly honest, knowledge that I needed to heal myself, too.

My authenticity and transparency while working with clients started to pay off. Clients were less hesitant to say yes; they were referring their friends and family and scheduling became a bit of a logistical challenge to fit everyone's sessions in. I saw clients fully; I saw not just what they were telling me but also things that they were not. My past career experience was becoming a resource: the ability to see between the lines of what clients were saying, the training as an officer of what body language cues to look for, the patience I had to wait without interruption as clients processed and proceeded with what they felt comfortable telling me, the ability to stay 100% neutral because nothing a client was about to tell me would shock me. This was refreshing to a lot of clients as many spent hundreds of hours in talk-therapy already. They were tired of talking about the details; they wanted to shift and be comfortable back in their own bodies. I was focused on shifting the learned behaviors of coping, deflecting, or numbing out, so they could come out of their shell and feel safe again.

As I became more and more booked, I quit my yoga teaching job so I could fully focus on building Tranquility Rising and shift towards fully becoming and truly being my own boss. As I refocused, I ended up getting more and more clients. It was as if clearing the energy of the safety net of teaching yoga unlocked a new level of trust within myself, and all my time slots were booked; first one week out, then two, then before I knew it people were booking months out to ensure they could see me every month. As long as I lived in my authenticity as a practitioner and continued to do this healing work, I stopped having to hustle and was able to be fully present for those who showed up to work with me. I was at ease as I leaned in and trusted what I'd created.

I get emotional looking back on this journey, because it takes strength, courage, and pushing through a lot of fears and self-doubt to choose the life of an entrepreneur. My spark was reignited on this path, and it would've been easy to stand behind the stability of what I had as a corrections officer, but the fire within me would not be tamed. It burned bright and I let it engulf me; I worked night and day staying true to my ultimate vision of not only becoming my own boss, but also building a holistic center of healing the physical, emotional, and spiritual bodies of those who seek it.

Today, Tranquility Rising has grown into a holistic center where several practitioners work in harmony for our clients with the same authenticity I started the business with. We know that it takes a team of wellness practitioners, because what works for one person might not work for another. At Tranquility Rising, we'll work to find the right path for you even if it isn't with us. It brings us joy to tap into this ancient wisdom passed down from teacher to teacher, and to be part of each client's journey.

Arielle Schmidt

Arielle Schmidt is the owner of Tranquility Rising in Cincinnati, Ohio. She is an ex-corrections officer turned holistic health practitioner providing SomaVeda® Thai Yoga Therapy with an added twist of Elemental Meridian Coaching. After years of working in a chronically stressful environment and living with trauma on a daily basis, she had the opportunity to take a month off and travel to India to restart her personal health and wellness journey, and to reconnect with herself. Her personal experience working as a corrections officer gave her a unique ability to understand and work with individuals (mostly women) who were looking for a deeper way to heal both physically and emotionally from their own trauma that traditional western therapies couldn't help them with. Her passion is to teach people to recognize that their physical pain could be connected to emotional blocks that result in tension in the body. She is acutely aware that when we bring awareness to these emotional blocks, it can drastically release what we hold in our bodies. SomaVeda® Thai Yoga Therapy is a combination of yoga assisted stretching, breath work, and acupressure to identify the blocks in the meridian channels. Arielle then takes the extra step to delve deeper by teaching the awareness of what the meridian channels mean to let clients take an active role in working outside of sessions.

In the start of 2020 with so many people being told to isolate, Arielle provided a safe and tranquil space to allow clients to receive bodywork when other massage therapists were forced to close their doors. In a time where uncertainty was high, she made it her mission to allow others to feel empowered with how they wanted to support their health. Moving through the next two years, Arielle expanded Tranquility Rising's studio space to incorporate other women holistic health practitioners to create a thriving community, all focused around client care and how clients choose to continue their healing journey.

Connect with Arielle:

linkedin.com/in/arielle-schmidt-9a3892113

2.

Energize Productivity and Put Distraction to Sleep!

Rachael Ansar | Owner of Monkey Puzzle Solutions, Organization & Productivity Consultant/Coach

Feeling utterly exhausted by the constant bombardment of distraction and never failing to select the most difficult route to get where I wanted to go was a familiar pattern in my life. Admittedly, most of the time, I eventually accomplished most of my goals, and the challenges I faced did, in fact, help build up my resilience and self-confidence. However, I often wish that I or someone else, had recognized my ADD tendencies earlier on in my life; maybe I would have had the support that I needed in selecting much easier and more enjoyable ways to achieve my goals. Instead, when growing up, I was often beaten down by people telling me I wasn't good enough or that I was too distracted and lacked the motivation needed to achieve. Even when I volunteered to have an ADD evaluation much later in my life, a psychologist asked me about my career goals. When I told him that one of my goals was to write a book, he laughed and responded by saying "Many people have that dream; give me a realistic goal that you can actually achieve!" Thankfully my own determination and love of helping people, along with my career choices in education/training, has helped shape the perfect foundation to begin my new business venture of consulting and coaching people who face similar organization and productivity challenges as I do.

In this chapter, we will briefly explore some of the key elements that contribute to a solid plan to manage time better and strive to be more productive in our approach. We will also look at some of the distractions that waste our time and threaten our success in "getting things done." The strategies offered in this chapter are common considerations that can increase our chances of accomplishing our daily tasks with a little more ease. For those of us who struggle to manage our time, find it difficult to stay focused, and often feel overwhelmed by all the chaos that surrounds us, we should not let our experiences cast doubt on the fact that we can learn the skills and develop the habits needed to make an impactful change in our lives. *My strength was once my weakness*! It is possible to enjoy a productive journey, minimize distractions, and allow ourselves to reach our desired destination with ease.

Take Action!

Let's start with one of the most respected leaders in the

organization and productivity industry, Stephen R. Covey. His words intend to remind all of us that we are the force that drives our actions.

"Be an agent, not a victim. Don't wait for life to happen to you; happen to it. Be the driver of your life, not a passenger. Live out of your imagination, not your past." [1]. He identifies how important it is for us to take action, by looking forward not backward. In agreement, it's our responsibility to attain personal/professional daily accomplishments or goals. If we are always looking backward, never forward, how can we possibly arrive at the desired destination? It is essential to identify and/or imagine what it is we want; however big or small that may be. Setting these goals enables us to become more deliberate with our time and processes. It doesn't have to be a painful journey. In fact, learning more productive approaches/habits provides us with the opportunity to experience a journey that positively satisfies our appetite every step of the way.

Perhaps we can relate to being a busy professional who is grappling with the constant bombardment of distractions, always rushing to complete daily tasks and projects in the hope that it does not affect the quality of our work and leave us feeling like we are forever drowning. Never leaving us a moment to come up for air and reflect on our successes or celebrate the reason why we choose our career path in the first place, let alone enjoy quality time with family. That dreaded feeling of being overwhelmed can prevent us from stepping up and making that much needed change. Knowing where to start can be one of the biggest challenges we encounter. Our first step in the right direction is identifying our vision of embracing a more productive approach in our lives and understanding why we need it. This will be our mantra needed to keep us going when we face mounting challenges that start to cloud our vision of what we are trying to achieve.

Identify the Essential

Next, it is important to consider Greg McKeown's *Essentialism: The Disciplined Pursuit of Less* (2014), a book that introduces us to a simple and effective technique.[2] He suggests that if we consistently ask ourselves if something is *essential*, we can let go of the rest, giving us permission to say "no" to tasks, projects, and activities that do not immediately lend themselves to what we are ultimately trying to achieve. If we are striving toward a more productive approach, this totally makes sense. When we are creating a daily plan, before adding a task, we simply ask McKeown's question: is it essential? Over time, we should find that we are able to reduce the amount of tasks that we are taking on. If we have more time in our schedule, we are not only opening up some wiggle room for tasks that may take longer than expected, we are also giving ourselves more time to enjoy what we do instead of rushing to get things done feeling hopelessly stressed and overwhelmed.

When we find ourselves successfully claiming back some of

our wasted time, we resist the urge to think of it as an opportunity to take on a heavier workload and continue to put ourselves under pressure. Think about how we can use this time for personal growth. Whenever I have an opening in my schedule, I use it to develop my skills in what I love to do – play the piano and complete my art projects. It is a welcomed break in my working day that I look forward to. It's like a celebration of completing my work tasks. A concept (The Pomodoro Technique) presented later in the chapter about rewarding yourself when you have completed a planned task with something you enjoy.[3]

Expect the Unexpected

I was fortunate enough to meet Emily Rogers, Owner of The Leap To Lead (who I would consider the most amazing coach who helped me identify and build my strengths in preparation for a new and exciting career). Nothing ever seemed to hinder her ability to accomplish daily tasks. As she explained to me one day, equal to exploring what is essential is anticipating "'the unexpected interruptions." She admits it is sometimes one of the biggest challenges that she faces when accomplishing her daily tasks. She understands the importance of planning or anticipating these types of interruptions in order to minimize their impact. For instance, working from home has its challenges. To give a specific example, if one of her children stays home from school because they are feeling unwell, her working day can still continue because she sets clear boundaries with her girls (granted that they are old enough to follow instructions while she works). They understand and respect that she works from home, therefore they have certain activities like reading, coloring, or craft projects that keep them busy while she works. Emily believes that her positive mindset and focusing on what she can do is key to the success of dealing with the unexpected and staying on track.

Conversely, if we share an office with someone, these types of distractions can be a little more challenging to resolve. If our job allows us to, and we can, take our work home, we can still go along with Emily's idea. However, if we work in a shared office and don't have the flexibility to take work home when faced with a challenge, unless a spouse or a family member is able to take care of our child(ren) at such short notice, it could possibly disrupt our whole day. In this instance, having a designated team member that could take on your essential tasks for that day would be great. This really reminds me of when I used to compete in chess tournaments. I couldn't possibly win a game without anticipating every possible move. Before committing to my next move, in my mind I would have to play out the next twenty possible moves my opponent could play in response to my next possible twenty moves. It sounds like a long and difficult, drawn out process, but over time it is almost like an automatic habit. However, my point is, if we anticipate distractions and some of these types of unexpected interruptions, we are in a much better position to accomplish what we want. Why? Because we are anticipating our counter moves or attacks.

Strategize Performance

A consideration that lends a great deal of value in creating a plan that works is identifying what part of the day in which we are most productive. If we identify that mid-morning is part of the day that we feel our energy is at its best, then on a regular basis, we should plan to complete the tasks that require more high-level executive functioning at that time. If we experience a lull in energy around mid-afternoon, then it makes sense for our daily plans to include the more menial tasks that do not require much focus, like scheduling appointments. Once we have identified a pattern of how we best perform and experience our varying levels of attention, we can plan accordingly to maximize results.

A useful exercise that enables us to reflect on how we currently use our time is to document what we do each day. If we do this for a couple of weeks, we can begin to identify patterns that remind us exactly of how we make good use of our time; and, conversely, it will highlight just how much time we are actually wasting. Furthermore, it will draw our attention to the types of distractions that easily mislead us. We can learn and better understand our strengths and weaknesses, providing us with crucial information to develop best strategies and nurture the habits needed to minimize disruption in our daily lives.

Multitasking vs. Multi-focusing

Additionally, McKeown raises an important point in understanding (*Essentialism*, 2014) "multitasking" vs. "multi-focusing." He explains that we can multitask quite easily. Listening to a podcast and eating our lunch at the same time supports this. However, we should not fool ourselves into believing that we can perform multiple tasks that require high-level executive function. For example, would it be possible to perform a surgical procedure and research an academic paper at the same time? Of course not.

The idea that we are unable to multi-focus was once challenged when I (reluctantly) accepted an opportunity to ride in the back seat of an aerobatic plane. It was fifteen of the most terrifying minutes of my life! Aside from the terror I experienced, it boggled my mind at just how much the pilot had to focus on. There was absolutely no room for error! While flying upward vertically, stalling the engine and falling out of the sky, then rolling continuously along a longitudinal axis, I had no idea where the earth was, nor the sky, and was just desperate to survive another five minutes. However, despite how this experience presented itself to me, the pilot reassured me later that it is a step-by-step process of learning and *practice* that enabled him to seamlessly execute each important task in sequence; and seemingly with ease. This was the confirmation needed for me to reaffirm that we don't actually multi-focus at the exact same time. It was in fact, a speedy succession of focused tasks. This was a detail easily missed. I did not see it as a broken down, step-by-step arrangement of perfectly performed functions.

Therefore, if we want to execute a task with precision, we must resist the urge to try and focus on more than one thing at a time. It isn't possible to focus on more than one thing at a time; however strong the urge might be. Sometimes it may appear like it is, with the aerobatic pilot for example, but that was a mastered performance of a highly practiced sequence of focused actions. If we foolishly try to consciously focus on more than one thing, it will only increase our chances of wasting time as we start to notice careless mistakes in our work. It only seemed that he was multi-focused because he was so skilled at what he was doing.

Renew our Focus

Up to this point, we have explored the benefits of committing to only what is essential; striving toward claiming back some of our wasted time by leaving behind the tasks that do not support our goals, allowing us a little more wiggle room to anticipate and plan for unexpected interruptions. Furthermore, we have a little more clarity on what types of tasks we can carry out unconsciously at the same time (managing our time more efficiently) and planning one high-level executive functioning task at a time.

However, do not misunderstand that we can now try to fill our schedules with as many tasks as possible. We need to set aside time for our well-being, to refuel mentally and physically; key components in driving the best outcome with quality results. This includes regular breaks in our daily routine. A small but impactful detail that is often forgotten. This too, if not included in our daily plan, will affect (negatively, mostly likely) our ability to get things done. As we don't always see and feel the immediate effects of taking regular breaks, it's easy to overlook.

Rob Dial (The Mindset Mentor) explains in his podcast ("Get S**t Done! - 6 Habits to Increase Productivity"), the Pomodoro Technique is an easy method to prevent mental fatigue.[4] He promotes this idea that taking regular breaks is crucial to producing our best work and performances. He goes on to explain, if we set a timer to go off after twenty-five minutes of being fully engaged in a work task, we should then take a five minute break (maybe grab a coffee); we can then return to what we were doing with a renewed sense of focus, with a better chance of sustaining the momentum needed to complete the task as planned. This can be repeated throughout the duration of the planned task. I use this technique, but slightly modified, when working from home. I start by putting my children's dirty laundry in the washing machine, knowing it takes forty-five minutes, then engage in my planned task knowing that in forty-five minutes my phone will notify me that the washing cycle has finished. That's when I take my next five-minute break to recharge and put in the next load of my never-ending dirty laundry piles. This is a habit I have successfully integrated while I work from home.

Minimize Distraction

We have established some considerations that can support us in our endeavor to become more productive. Now we will look at some of the distractions that terrorize our efforts in getting things done and explore possible ways to minimize their impact. For some, distractions can be the biggest enemy of productivity. A daily battle that impacts our time and diminishes any sense of being in control of our schedules or tasks. Exploring some of those distractions and solutions that can be integrated in our daily routines can help us regain control of our time.

Our own thoughts and fleeting ideas can often be responsible for intercepting our drive and focus. A swift way of dealing with these unwanted distractions is to record the thought or idea in a physical notebook or digital note-taking app to later decide on its worth or final destination. This is an action that should not take long at all. It allows our minds to let go of the thought or idea in order to return to what we were doing minimizing the impact. Microsoft's OneNote is a great note-taking app that is free and packed with features to aid our time management. Information can easily be transferred to other apps and does not require a subscription. Evernote, another popular note-taking app, has some excellent features to sort and organize in a more customized way. Recording thoughts and ideas also helps if you don't have a great memory – like me!

Not surprisingly, digital distractions can be the most

troublesome contributors to disengaging us from our everyday tasks and activities. For some of us, it can be a very real problem and issue. Not only can it impede our ability to complete projects on time, it challenges our ability to estimate how long a task may actually take to complete. This develops a pattern that diminishes our self-confidence.

A common example of this distraction causing more disruption than intended is hearing a notification sound (one of many) on our mobile phone that is attempting to alert us. Immediately, this grabs our attention and we cannot deny the urge to take a five-minute sneaky-peak (as we immediately justify this momentary lapse in judgment by reassuring ourselves that we need a break anyway). Of course it's nothing important, it's just someone on our neighborhood Facebook page posting a question asking where the nearest beach is to our neighborhood (located in Denver, Colorado). What? A little confused by this question, I can't resist figuring out how long it would actually take to drive to a beach from where we live (which, by the way, would take approximately 22.30 hours. In case you were wondering...). Thirty-five minutes later, I realized I had fallen victim to being sucked into the endless abyss of social information that didn't contribute to my day at all; but rather, it actually hijacked my valuable time. We need to catch ourselves before participating in activities such as this and ask that important question – "Is it essential I respond to the notification right now?" This is an obvious way to self-talk our way out of allowing the notification to side track us. If we plan designated time to check our social media platforms, we can simply acknowledge that we will check it later during that designated time; rather than letting it steal our valuable time and attention and suck us into the abyss of distraction.

As we are well aware, emails or platforms we use for communication are essential for the work that we do. However, when we hear an email alert, it can often be an unwelcome distraction because ultimately we know that not only does it require our attention, it's probably about to claim even more of our time. Personally, to prevent this type of distraction from disrupting my work, I switch off all notifications on my phone and laptop throughout the day while I work. I check my emails twice a day (when I want) and my phone line remains open in case my children or their schools are trying to contact me. I cannot stress enough how much this has provided me with a sense of control over my time and it has given back some much needed time that I once wasted just trying to keep up with the constant flow of emails. I even feel more engaged with what I do now. This is just a small, but very impactful adjustment! Obviously, this may not work with everyone and how they operate, but it can certainly be a consideration that may be modified to suit a more productive approach.

Be Present

Additionally, we often experience a love-hate relationship with our mobile phone. Whether we are easily affected by distraction or not, it's easy to pick up our phone and completely disconnect ourselves from what's going on around us. How many of us have been sitting at a restaurant table with our colleagues or friends (no judgment here, as I've done it several times myself) and picked up our phones to check something that probably could have waited? It can be, and usually is, a subconscious habit. We aren't *trying* to disengage with our social life and guests. It's a habit. Maybe we can agree that resisting this allows us to be fully engaged with our colleagues/friends. Being present can only be a good thing for everyone involved, right? It would be great if it was a subconscious habit *not* to check our phones. Consider how it looks and feels *for you* if someone is frequently checking their phones across the table, as opposed to someone who stays connected and engaged throughout the event.

I remember many years ago, before I had children, I forgot my mobile phone when I went away on vacation. I was horrified when I made the discovery, I felt as if I had left part of myself back at home. How was I going to think, or function, without it?! Unexpectedly, it was possibly the best vacation that I have ever experienced. I have never felt so present in all my life. No one could reach me even if they tried. The next two weeks (336 hours to be exact) were entirely mine. I felt totally and utterly cut off from the outside world. It was glorious! I can't imagine leaving for vacation now and discovering I do not have my phone with me (but this is more because I have children to worry about). The world has conditioned us to feel like we are dependent on our phones and we will not miss a beat if we stay connected.

Environmental Impact

Aside from digital distractions, another consideration would be to look at the environment/space that we work in. We can make a simple assessment by checking the area for possible distractions that may be impeding our productivity. For example, if we work in a cluttered space, then it may be beneficial to include in our daily plan to tidy up at the end of each working day in order to begin the next day in a clean space, and on the right foot. A cluttered space clutters the mind, and a clear space clears the mind! Makes sense, doesn't it?! If we maintain this, which we all know can be a challenge, we should keep reminding ourselves why we are doing it. Even for a small step like this, it helps to "Begin with the end in mind." [5] Covey believes that if you begin each task by envisioning the desired outcome, you are essentially sowing the seed, opening up a clearer path to get there. If something feels like a chore, use this technique of reminding ourselves why we are doing it. It helps motivate us to commit and practice the habits needed to support our journey.

If we are lucky enough to have a designated office space at home, even the position of our desk can impact our work. For example, if I had a desk facing a window that looked out toward a small fishing village with a beach trailing off into the distance, I'd quite literally get nothing done. Ever. I would constantly find myself caught in a daydream searching for the perfect spot to magically teleport myself to. However, if I had my back to the window and the door closed to avoid other visual distractions, I'd be more likely to sail through my daily work tasks.

A Quiet Space

Furthermore, depending on the level of focus needed to accomplish a task, I either like to listen to some relaxing background music to drown out the audio distractions outside of my working space, or when I need to engage in something that requires high-level executive functioning, I need *total silence*. Admittedly, that is not always possible. I often have a Plan B because I have two toddlers running around the house a lot of the time when I am at home trying to work. If my husband, who works remotely too, is not available to entertain them, I need to have activities readily available for my little ones to keep them occupied while I complete my work tasks. There has been the odd time when I have had to run off to the local library to claim a quiet space. It takes a lot of juggling to make it work. As long as we have options included in our plan, we can make it happen with a little more ease rather than allow it to throw you off track.

Perhaps, we work in a shared office space surrounded by other distractions like nearby conversations, colleagues striking up a conversation about problems they are experiencing, multiple ring tones heard in the background or colleagues simply moving about going about their daily tasks too. At first glance, it may seem like an impossibility to claim a quiet space amongst everything going on. Our resilience is key to stay on track; while continuing to remember our goal to be more productive. If we are able to identify an alternative area to temporarily work in when we need to avoid distraction, we can seek the support of our team and hope that they respect the space we need. If finding an alternative space is unrealistic, we can turn to the possibility of wearing headphones (with or without music playing) to either dampen out the distracting sounds, or send a subtle visual message to others that we are engaged in our work and wish not to be interrupted. It often takes the help of others to achieve what we need to accomplish. Isn't this what teamwork is all about?! Maybe, together with our colleagues, we can come up with something fun, but effective, that allows us to feel in control of our time and not falling victim to someone else claiming our time. Our efforts to support one another builds team camaraderie.

Connect the Dots with a Journal

Last, but certainly not least, journaling is a great way to boost productivity. Though it can often feel like a chore, it is one of the most effective ways to become more productive. This has certainly been the case for me personally. It goes above and beyond just writing down the activities of our day. It records and tracks our progress when writing about how and what we want to accomplish. We are able to see what is compromising our efforts and catch it before it becomes an overwhelming challenge to correct. Recording and reflecting on how something didn't quite work helps identify alternative solutions, ultimately building our resilience and self-confidence. It empowers a continuous sense of self-improvement. A journal highlights opportunities that may otherwise be forgotten. It reminds us to celebrate our accomplishments, something that is needed to fuel our motivation to continue toward a more productive path. There are endless reasons why a journal is beneficial. Our brains are unruly when it comes to hiding useful information – personally, if I don't write something down, there's a very big chance it will get lost in that reservoir of information that we call our subconscious; likely never to be found again. When we develop the habit of documenting and reflecting at the end of each day, we increase the chances of connecting the dots, boosting our ability to recall memories that serve our pursuit in accomplishing what we need to do to fulfill our goals. Thus, everything becomes more clear, supporting our need to maintain a more productive approach.

Better System, Better Habits

It's easy to find and explore solutions to help in and with our quest in avoiding daily distractions that diminish our ability to work towards a more productive approach. However, if we strive *to turn some of these solutions into habits* (that we frequently practice) we will have a better chance of creating the change needed to *maintain* a system that works and less likely to deviate and go back to what was once an overwhelming challenge. "If you are having trouble changing your habits, the problem isn't you. The problem is your system. Bad habits repeat themselves again and again not because you don't want to change, but because you have the wrong system for change." [6] Clear makes an important point here. When we apply his idea to feeling stuck in a never ending cycle of distraction and time that we feel like we cannot manage, we should not blame ourselves, but rather, understand that we are likely feeling like this is because we do not have an adequate system or plan to make the necessary change. When we learn ways to minimize the distraction that affect us, and skills to manage time better, we successfully implement those skills. We need to include those skills in our daily plan/routine, eventually they provide us with the frequent opportunity to practice our new identified system, developing new, good habits that replace old, "bad" ones. In support of this, we should never lose sight of why we are striving toward making these changes. Our success depends on it! Just remember that it is *normal* to backslide and nearly impossible for us to maintain a perfectly organized and productive approach at *all* times. And that is okay! We must strive to let go of this expectation of perfection and recognize that perfection is not our goal here. Progress is. We should set realistic expectations that sometimes we will allow distractions or unexpected interruptions to disrupt our daily plans despite everything we have put in place to help us accomplish. Part of our journey is to develop the resilience and self-confidence to get right back on track. It's an *ongoing* process that productivity requires. As many industry leaders will say: organization and productivity is a process not an event. Quite often, it takes a more informed understanding of the true nature of what we struggle with to take that leap forward in attaining success.

To Summarize:

In order to manage our time better and minimize distractions, it is crucial to develop a new system or approach to accomplish our tasks on a daily basis. We are the driving force behind change in our lives. Therefore, an easy place to begin would be creating a vision of what a more productive system would look like (as this vision will be a reminder to motivate our journey to lead us in the right direction and stay on track). Filtering out what is only essential allows us to claim back wasted time and daily planning becomes much easier to navigate. If we anticipate unexpected interruptions as we have encountered in the past, we can create a plan to prevent them from derailing our journey. Furthermore, recognizing the level of focus needed to complete any given task, can be planned at a time during the day that matches our energy levels, to complete with quality and precision. We can identify and learn ways to minimize the impact of daily distractions and turn them into positive habits that maintain new systems supporting our pursuit in managing our time better. Using a journal and recording our progress throughout the day can help us recognize the solutions that best suit us; additionally, it can help us identify and develop effective ways to implement and maintain them.

Remember, if our goal is to be more productive with our time, just think of it as an on-going process, not an event!

Notes

1. (Covey, Stephen R..The 7 Habits of Highly Effective People, 2020, pg. 107)
2. McKeown, Greg. Essentialism: The Disciplined Pursuit of Less, New York, Crown Publishing, 2014.
3. Cirrillo, Francesco. The Pomodoro Technique, francescocirillo.com/pages/pomodoro-technique
4. Dial, Rob. 2020, October 19. "Get S**t Done! - 6 Habits to Increase Productivity" (The Mindset Mentor Podcast), retrieved from spotify.com
5. Covey, Stephen R.. The 7 Habits of Highly Effective People, New York, Simon & Schuster, 2020, pg 111
6. Clear, James. Atomic Habits, New York, Avery, 2018, pg. 252

Rachael Ansar

Rachael is a member of the National Association of Productivity & Organizing Professionals and owner of Monkey Puzzle Solutions. Originally from the UK, she has been living in the US for more than a decade with her husband and three children. Her business provides consultancy and coaching services aimed to help people who feel overwhelmed. Rachael helps clients to build the skills and habits needed to successfully implement organized and more productive approaches in managing busy lifestyles or businesses. Her passion for coaching, finding creative solutions, and resourcefulness empowers her clients to approach their personal or professional goals with clarity.

As a young adult, Rachael found it difficult to focus. She remembers struggling to jump in feet first when a new and exciting opportunity was discovered and supported her goals. Rachael soon realized a familiar pattern of feeling swamped by disorganization and chaos, preventing her from completing a task or project that she knew that she was perfectly capable of achieving. Often starting with a keen interest to get stuck-in, that feeling would soon turn to dread, allowing distraction to take over. Rachael's determination and career choices provided her with an opportunity to transform her struggles into successes.

Professionally, Rachael has worked for more than two decades in training and educational roles across a diverse range of industries and learning abilities, working with people from toddlers to retirees. Throughout her career she has discovered her passion for helping people to learn more effectively based on their individual learning styles. Teaching became a platform to develop creative solutions that help people successfully accomplish their educational goals. Through her fast-paced career, ten years at home managing her busy family, and achieving her never-ending list of professional and personal goals have all contributed to the creation of her company: Monkey Puzzle Solutions.

Connect with Rachael:

linkedin.com/in/rachaelansar

https://www.monkeypuzzlesolutions.com/

3.

The Evolution of a Networking Introvert

Angel Hicks | Visionary & CEO | Collaboration Specialist | Speaker | Trainer

Eight years ago, I was thrust into professional networking. I didn't stumble into it or realize I needed it by hearing someone else's success. I wasn't recommended to try it by a caring friend. I was, quite literally, thrust into it.

I was a single mom of three kids working fifty hours a week at a dead-end job. After months of complaining (you know…not doing anything about it but complaining to my Mom), she decided to introduce me to a man who owned a local networking group called The Business Network (now known as H7 Network).

At first I was like "No way. I'm going to die happy and alone, Mom. I don't want to date because the pool is poisonous." Her response? "Just meet the guy! He may know people who are hiring for sales. He's got a huge network and may be able to find you a new job." Okay, that sounds a little more rational.

So a few weeks before Christmas, Clay and I met for a one-to-one. I made my mother go with me (I swore this was not going to turn into a date!) and we hit it off. Of course, lightning struck us both and three months later we were engaged; and six months after that we were married. I truly did not see that coming. I always say if you want to hear God laugh, tell him your plan! A year and a half after we were married, I took over the one women's group in TBN and started Evolve Women's Network.

In this chapter, my goal is to give you tools to use to not only create a plan for professional networking success, but also to give you tools to use to be more effective and efficient in your entrepreneurial journey. Let's do this!

When I first started networking, I had no idea what networking was. I was a super shy wallflower-introvert who could barely speak in front of a room let alone present an entire elevator pitch. But I was married to the founder so I kind of had to figure it out. I *wanted* to figure it out. I knew I was being called to grow outside of the tiny box I had created for myself. I was going to suffocate inside my comfort zone if something didn't change.

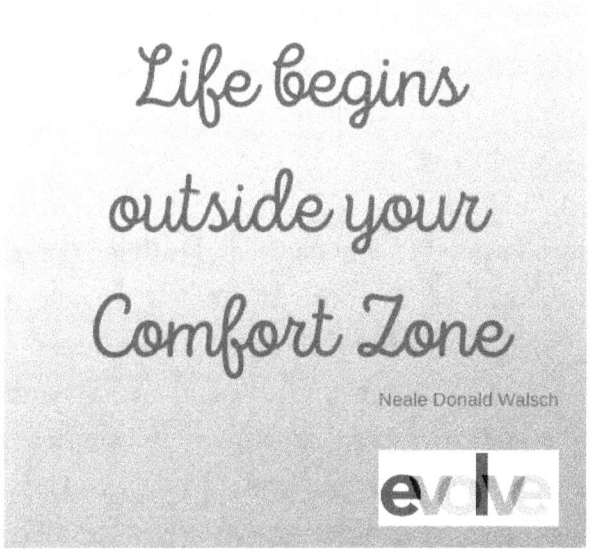

It took me more than a few times in front of the group before I started growing in confidence and being able to explain who I was and what I did. Before long, I found myself on the leadership team, creating presentations, and stretching and challenging who I thought I was. I have always believed that self awareness is one of the greatest gifts you will receive in your lifetime but you're the only one that can provide that for yourself. Clarity comes from action, not thought. The more I got out in front, the more I fell in love with presenting information and watching the light bulbs go off for the people in front of me. I started presenting on topics such as LinkedIn, Social media marketing, networking strategies, and back-office organization. All of the skills I was using for my clients became opportunities to share my expertise and the knowledge I was learning.

One of the biggest revelations I had from the early stages of my self-awareness journey was the difference between an introvert and an extrovert. Being an introvert versus. An extrovert isn't a popularity contest. It's simply where you get your energy from. Where do you feel energized and where do you feel drained? As an introvert, I can stay in my house for days. A good book, a good bottle of red wine, the internet, and my husband is really all I need to feel joyful and fulfilled. I feel energized when I'm alone. I feel drained when I'm around a lot of people for long periods of time. As I grew in confidence, I also grew in my joy of being around a lot of people and could go longer and longer in a social setting or environment. I used to present a workshop and then pull into my driveway realizing I've never even turned on my radio. I was drained! The greatest part about this realization was I figured out that I wasn't broken. I was just different…and that was okay. I had to learn how to manage my introversion. Now I can be around a lot of people for extended periods of time without crashing afterwards.

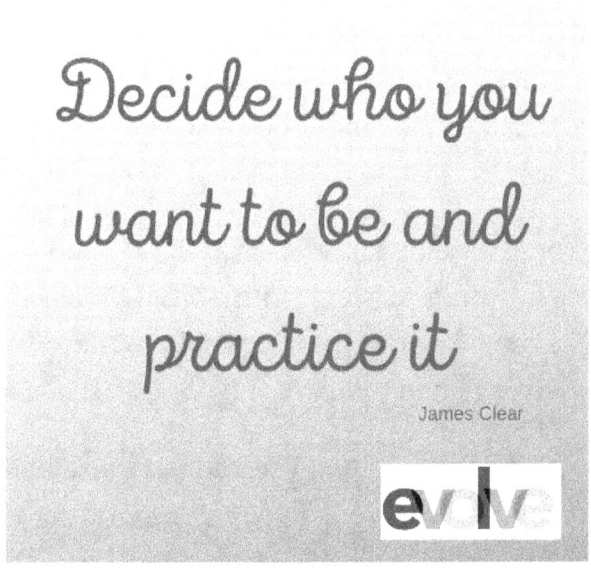

These are a few tips I learned during my evolution into becoming a networking pro.

1. Don't go into networking to sell to the room! Learn to sell through the room.

I remember when I had launched a brand new business called Sassy Pros to help busy entrepreneurs fill in the gaps between their passion and running their business by providing executive assistance in-house as well as virtually. I couldn't wait to start networking. My whole goal was to sell my services to the people in the room. After all, each of them could use my services and needed me, right? They were all my ideal clients! They were like kids in a candy story. I wanted them all! *facepalm*

I was so wrong.

I was trying to sell *to the room*. While, yes, there may be someone in the room that may need your services, **the goal of professional networking is to know, like, and trust** the people in the room. You don't just get it because you're in the same room.

The people in the room already knew what I did. If you feel you need to convince others to work with you, they aren't your ideal client(s). They will find you if (and when) they are ready. This was something I had to learn.

When you try to sell to the people in the room, two things can happen. One, they become your clients. Yay! You have a service or product they find valuable. Kudos. The second scenario is much worse. They smell that sales tactic from a mile away and want nothing to do with you. They don't refer to you because all you do is try to sell to them. You're constantly trying to convince them that your magic potion or solution is the one! People love to buy things, but no one likes to be sold.

It's important to remember that what we're actually doing in that room is educating others. We're building relationships. We're serving them without expecting anything in return. Relationships take time. They are mutually beneficial. If you're in the room and are struggling to obtain referrals or connections, take a look at *why* you're in the room.

As for those future clients of yours, here's something to think about: If you feel the need to convince others to work with you, they aren't your ideal client. They will find you if (and when) they are ready.

2. Learn how to start, and carry, a conversation

As a shy introvert, I used to hate small talk. I wasn't good at it and the anxiety when the inevitable awkward silence would hit was just a nightmare for me because, as it turns out, other people aren't great at small talk either. I learned a technique from my husband when I was first starting out. This technique has served me at dinners with members and their spouses, ball games with other parents, backyard BBQs, and, of course, at networking events of all kinds. These are great questions to keep in your back pocket for those times when you need to start, and hold, a conversation.

5 Questions to Ask when getting to know someone:

1. **What do you do?** I know this seems elementary. But we are trying to be active listeners and even though I know what a realtor, insurance agent, or plumber does, I want to hear what they say they do. You will learn much more about them if you're interested in what they say they do versus you assuming you already know what they do.
2. **Where are you from?** You will be amazed at the commonality that can come from this question. Finding commonality is one of the easiest ways to connect with others. This question can also lead to more questions and more conversation.
3. **Tell me about your family.** I no longer ask them to tell me about their husband or kids. I asked a woman once,

who was in her mid to late thirties, to tell me about her husband and kids. Tears welled up in her eyes and she said that was the one thing she was never blessed with. I cried with her...and will never forget the awkwardness that followed. I never made that mistake again. When you say "Tell me about your family" you will have grown women talking about their dogs, men talking about their grandkids...never mentioning that they have their own kids! This gives them the freedom to tell you what's important to them. Never assume the relationship status of someone sitting across from you or assume what's important to them.

4. **What do you do for fun?** This one is my favorite! Did you know there is a group of ballroom dancers who teach people with special needs how to dance? I didn't either! This woman said she had never been in a room with such joyful people. You'll find out about all kinds of cool things that people do, maybe some you didn't even know were a thing!

5. *Last but not least for your business connections,* **How can I help you? What keeps you up at night in your business? What do you struggle with the most?** All of these questions help you help them. A lot of people don't know how you can help them. It's your job to earn their trust and helping someone else is a sure way to do that.

3. Search for others sitting alone

The first time I went to a chamber of commerce event I was so intimidated! I hadn't yet learned to get to the event early and when I walked into the meeting, almost everyone was already in a circle. They were chatting as if they were old friends. The tables were full of people connecting, laughing, and passing around business cards. I was like a fish out of water. I couldn't breathe. My eyes were darting around the room trying to find an escape route. Mere seconds before I turned around and walked out, I spotted another woman sitting alone. Her head was down looking at her phone and there was an empty seat next to her. I made a bee line for that seat! I spotted that fellow introvert from across the room and I was clinging to her for dear life. I have been her. I sat in that same seat looking at my phone as if what it was communicating was a matter of life or death. What it is actually communicating is "I don't want to look like I'm miserable and awkward and alone, so I'm going to act like something important is on this thing." When I got to that open seat, I said "Excuse me, I don't think we've met." I stuck out my hand for a good old fashioned hand shake. She took it and introduced herself and a new connection was made. Boom! We were no longer alone.

*Tip: When entering a new arena, look for others who are sitting alone. More than likely they are looking for a lifeline too. They feel awkward and nervous. Feeling alone in a room full of other humans is the most isolating feeling. Make it a point to rescue others. Once you know, you know.

4. Get there early!

One of the best tips for introverts I can share is to get there early. Getting to an event early gives you the opportunity to scope out the place and get comfortable. Check out where the bathroom is, where the best seat is, meet the facilitator, etc. This has given me the opportunity to select my table and seat before everyone is already in their own cliques. I also ask the facilitator if there's anything I can do to help. They almost always say yes! Facilitators are often overwhelmed on the day of an event so getting there a little early and asking how you can help is a great way to not only be helpful (obviously), but then the facilitator will often introduce you to others who are helping at the event. In my experience, asking the facilitator if I can help at an event where I don't know a soul is the easiest way to meet new people quickly. They also always remember you, so you're increasing your influence and your network at the same time. Win-Win.

5. Learn to break up the crowd. Horseshoe is the shape to be.

This one can be a tough one for the shy introverts in the room. Outgoing extroverts eat this up, but for others it may take some getting used to. Have you ever walked into a professional event and everyone is already standing around in circles? There are a dozen circles and everyone is just having a grand time? Meanwhile you don't know a single person and even if you do, they're talking already so you feel weird and alone and you're left wondering what to do. Here's a trick that I use and have taught many attendees. First of all, if you're the one standing in the circle, do us all a solid and take a step back to turn your body outward. When you stand in the closed circle, you're telling everyone in the room that anyone who should be in the circle already is. There's no room here for anyone else. Be the change, open the circle and let others in! If you're looking to join the circle, pick something physical that you can compliment on someone else. Maybe it's their shoes, scarf, tie, or pin you find a connection to. Here's what I say: "Excuse me, I'm so sorry to interrupt. I don't think we've met before but I couldn't help but notice your (dress, shoes, pin, tie.) It's beautiful (awesome, cool, I went there too)!" Their response, as they move to open the circle, "Oh no worries. Thank you so much! I got it _____. This is Tom, Dave, Marcy, and Janet. What do you do?" And *boom* I'm in. All it took was for me to be nice to someone else. This may sound like a self-serving compliment, but really it's a win-win. They get a compliment, the group meets someone new, and I'm not stuck standing by myself. Boom! (Are you noticing a Win-Win theme?)

6. Learn how to confidently introduce yourself.

Okay, so we know that I was a shy introvert when I started networking. I could barely utter my name and after a few weeks of listening to others introduce themselves, I finally got the courage to introduce myself. That first introduction was horrific. I forgot what I did, I fumbled through what I thought the group wanted to hear, and subsequently vowed on that day that I would never fumble through describing myself again. No one who was there that day even remembers what I said. They only remember how I made them feel, which is good because I felt like an idiot. I had to learn to confidently introduce myself. I listened to many other members' commercials, found other members of the group to bounce ideas off of, and ended up with a decent commercial.

But I wasn't confident in my skill-set. I had to really dig deep to figure out what I was actually good at, what I was an expert in, and why I did what I did. Once I was able to tell my story to the group, not just what I did but *why* I did it, I gained new confidence and new clients.

If you struggle like I did to really understand your talents, I have an exercise for you. Write down every job you have ever had. Yes, even that time you worked at that United Dairy Farmer's gas station for that summer. Then write down three skills or lessons you learned at each job. What did you take away from the experience? How did it shape who you are today? I was the first person to get a tip at my job at UDF. It was a dollar from the coach of a baseball team and I learned that a genuine smile goes a long way. All of those little lessons have molded you to the person you are today. Bask in the glory of who you are, what you know, and lessons you can teach others. Remember you are beautiful, you are kind, and you are smart. Introduce yourself as such.

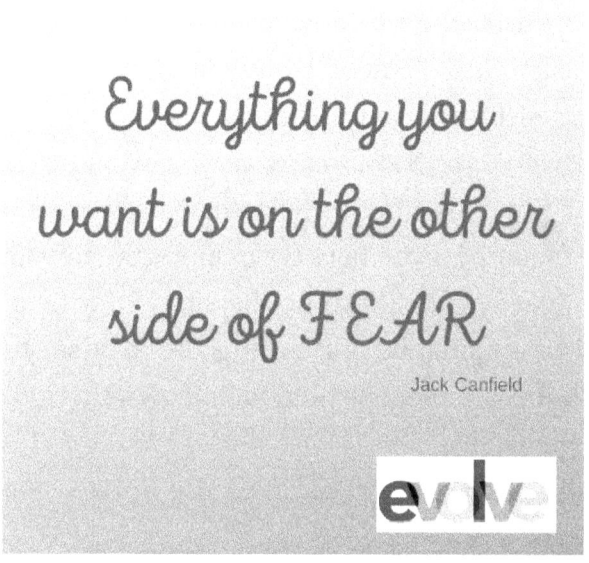

7. Create a team

When you first start your business, you are the IT department, the marketing manager, the operations officer…you're all the things. The success or failure of your business relies on *you and only you*. Period. When you're out networking, meeting all of these amazing professionals, start a spreadsheet (or use a Customer Relationship Management program) of all of the people you meet. Who did you really connect with? Who seems like they would be willing to be helpful? Who has a service you would like to utilize now or in the future? Start to create your team of experts that you can call when you get stuck. Professional networking should have a mentor/mentee mentality. We should be willing to help one another without expecting anything in return. Align with those who are like-minded and don't hesitate to reach out if you need help. Every time I go to a room with professional networkers and I ask, "How many of you would answer the call of another person in this room if they reached out for help?" Every hand went up. "How many of you would give them some of your precious time to help them overcome a challenge they are facing? Maybe help them move the needle and get unstuck?" Every hand stayed up. Reach out for help! We live in a world of abundance and having the mindset to lean on others, ask for, and accept help will allow others to lean on you.

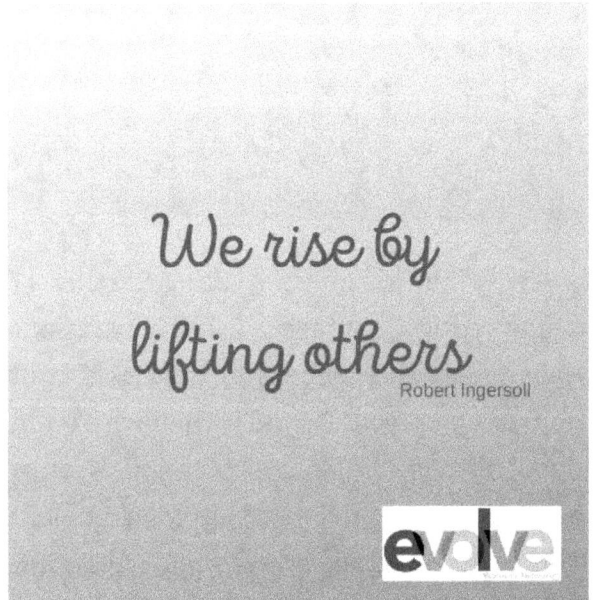

Over the last eight years of networking, growing my business, and growing myself, I have learned so many lessons that help to serve others. I'm sure you have too. Here are a few more tips that I use as an entrepreneur to make my days more productive.

1. Time blocking and the Pomodoro Technique

We can't manage time, we can only manage ourselves. When you start your business no one is there to tell you what to do (thankfully!). There are no deadlines, no clocking in or out, or daily tasks set before you. You have to figure that out on your own. I use time-blocking to help me achieve work/life harmony. I stop working every day at 3:00 p.m. and only work half days on Friday. I take the weekends completely off, unless it's an emergency, and I barely have my phone on me. Time-blocking my week allows me to have appointments when I want them, get the back-office things in my business done, and still have time for myself. It gives me direction and keeps me on task.

The Pomodoro technique is something I learned from a client with ADHD. You set your timer for twenty-five minutes and set about completing one task. Take a five minute break. (Dance break anyone?!) Set it again for twenty-five minutes. Repeat up to four times. Once the task is complete, take a thirty minute break. I don't use this for *everything*, but when there is a task that I don't want to do or that takes a lot of brain power, this technique is a game changer for me. I also use my timer to answer emails, make calls, anything that I tend to get easily distracted with or carried away with.

2. Dance breaks

It's proven that dancing increases blood flow and vibration. Moving my body several times a day to the beat of music is a balm to my soul. Create a YouTube playlist with all of your favorite upbeat tunes. May I suggest "This is Me" from *The Greatest Showman* soundtrack? Seriously life changing.

3. Take time to connect to a higher power

Whether you believe in God, the Universe, or Source Energy, get quiet and get to know yourself. I am a faith-based believer and believe that God is my creator. I have had many quiet conversations with God, and when I'm done, I don't hear a thing. No answers, no parting of the clouds, no big "Dad" voice to tell me what's the best course of action. But inevitably sometime in the near future, I have a conversation with someone who gives me the answer. Or sheds light on my questions. Or gives me a new way of thinking about my problem. And, thus, a new solution.

If you are not currently taking fifteen to thirty minutes a day to have a board meeting with a Higher Self, pen that in stone now. Every day, that is your first priority. God is a sounding board, He will give you what you are seeking. It just may not come the way you think it's going to. Be on the lookout for the answers you seek. They are all around you...most of them are in you.

> *You are confined only by the walls you build yourself.*
>
> — evolve

When you're out professionally networking, whether you're new or seasoned, introverted or extroverted, the sole purpose is to build relationships. Some of these connections and relationships will evolve into true friendships, collaborations, or referral partners. Remember to educate others on *why* you do what you do; don't just try to sell them on *what* you do. You are your brand. Earning like, know, and trust with your network will give you unlimited opportunities for many years to come.

Today, I am the CEO and founder of Evolve Women's Network. Evolve is a women's networking and entrepreneurial support group. We have two rules: no cliques and no judgment. We're all just squirrels trying to get a nut. Some of us have more nuts than others, but it doesn't change the nature of the squirrel. If we can link arms, get off the entrepreneurial island, and climb in the boat together, we all rise. Rising tides lift all boats and WE are the rising tides.

If you feel alone in your journey or would just like to be a part of a group of like-minded women, feel welcome to check out www.EvolveWomensNetwork.com and join us for a meeting. There's a seat waiting for you.

Angel Hicks

Angel Hicks is the CEO & Founder of Evolve Women's Network. She and her husband own two networking organizations, H7 Network and Evolve. Angel has spent her twenty-five year career in small business; and, in 2016, she took over a small women's group in Cincinnati. Angel has spent the last five years growing Evolve from that one location in Cincinnati to six locations spanning three states! She also has added weekly international virtual meetings with over 300 members attending. She prides herself in building relationships first and creating collaboration over competition. Evolve Women's Network is where "Connections become Community ©. Evolve was recognized in "Cincy Chic's" Best of Cincinnati for the best women's networking group in 2020.

Angel is a self professed "networking introvert." When she first started as an entrepreneur, she could barely share her own commercials, let alone present in front of a group. When the opportunity arose for her to take over a women's networking group, she was reluctant. After thoughtful prayer, she decided to accept the challenge. She joined the leadership team of her local chapter of H7 Network, moving up to a director's position, then into operations, and finally as the President of H7. During this time, she started presenting on a wide range of subjects, practicing her speaking skills, and gaining recognition as a speaker and trainer.

After many years of practice and perseverance, she has had numerous opportunities to present at colleges, local chambers, and other networking groups. She is now a DISC Certified trainer, (DISC is a personality assessment similar to the Enneagram or Myers Briggs's personality assessments) and often trains on the DISC personality analysis as well as networking success techniques, and LinkedIn workshops. She is passionate about encouraging other women to understand themselves and Live Life Out Loud!

Connect with Angel:

linkedin.com/in/angelhicks

4.

You are the Creator of Your Success

Melissa Kirkpatrick |Motivational Speaker | Transformational Business & Life Coach

Whether you're a business owner or an entrepreneur, imagine being in the same spot you are in five years from now. Are you struggling, stressed out, wishing, and hoping for things to change because you are uncertain about what to do next? Do you watch others as they succeed, feeling frustrated and wondering what they have and what you don't?

The truth is that business is complicated no matter who you are or what you do. Doing it all on your own can feel like treading water or trying to climb out of quicksand. Business owners have the motivation and excitement but often lack the clarity and support needed to grow successfully.

Does this sound familiar? Then you are in the right place.

With this chapter, I intend to offer you some guidance and understanding of moving past what feels like failing and how to step boldly into a successful life and business. You will learn practical tips to apply so you can move forward faster.

Let's begin with a secret.

I learned this secret personally and saw how others had the same problem. I knew it kept stopping others in their pursuit of growth and success in business. It has been proven many times over with clients and me. What I now understand to be the number one secret to growing a successful business is to get out of your damn way and do the work! No one is coming to save you. You are the creator of your success.

I know that sounds a little harsh, but that's the reality.

Here are three identifiers I found when someone is getting in their way of doing business:

- You begin creating barriers and walls with your thoughts that keep you stuck and stalled by not accepting help because of your ego.
- You cannot figure out how to grow your business and make more money, although you've tried and spent thousands of dollars unsuccessfully.
- Your confidence and clarity to focus on your goals is exhausting, and quitting isn't an option but sure seems like a better plan.

Can you relate?

The struggle is real, and being stuck and stalled in your business only delays scaling and growing. The clarity came for me when my family owned two public golf courses. Before that, I was a high school teacher; my true passion in life is teaching.

I left teaching when we bought the golf courses. I continued educating others by developing a program for coordinating women's golf sessions. I likened lessons on and off the course with a program called Find Your Own D.R.I.V.E.

Behind the scenes, though, the stress of owning a family-run business became too much, and I turned to alcohol to cope.

I soon realized I wasn't living what I was teaching.

Once I released the problem, which was getting in my way by self-destructing my success with the use of alcohol and not making the best decisions, I saw a way out.

I stopped drinking, put on my C.E.O. hat, and got clear. I launched my true calling, a service, using my personal and professional experiences.

I was ready and willing to show up for myself, appreciate and be grateful for opportunities. I was ready to embrace being a successful business owner.

My question for you is: **"If you could find solutions to your problems, and show up with clear intentions to do the work, would you get out of your way and accept the help?"**

Of course!

Now let's help you flip the focus so you can align with solutions and not problems!

Begin by equipping yourself with the right tools and strategies to be grateful and happy by determining how to release the feelings of being overwhelmed, frustrated, and stressed. This is critical.

Coaching Tip #1: *Knowledge is power!*

Identify what makes you feel overwhelmed, frustrated, and stressed. Acknowledge how you may be masking those feelings with drinking, overeating, spending money, not sleeping, smoking, etc. – to name a few.

From this awareness, you can process the emotions attached to the feelings and behaviors. Write out on paper those categories of emotions you want to overcome and begin by asking for each emotion:

"What is the emotion I'm feeling?"

"How am I creating these feelings?"

"Why do I believe holding onto this emotion is good for me?"

*Note: Don't be surprised if you discover that it is usually related to an experience from your past or some belief you've received from others for holding onto this emotion.

Once you can shine a light on the emotions and trust that it's only a thought, and a thought can be changed, you can reach for a better feeling.

What I discovered in doing this work was my fear that my parents would no longer love me if I were unsuccessful. Growing up, there was an apparent belief and preconceived notions surrounding money. Those comments of "the rich get richer, while the poor get poorer" and strong jealousy for those who were wealthy were beliefs I took on as genuine.

From a young age, my goal was to be prosperous! And I was doing just that until the fear of an underlying belief from my upbringing caused me to self-sabotage in a way that I would not be successful.

Not surprisingly, as I researched successful entrepreneurs, many have been down this road and came out on the other side. It was helpful for me to see that I wasn't alone.

As mentioned in the previous section, there were some challenges that I struggled with, not only with alcohol but overeating and overspending. Identifying these challenges and having the support of my own business and a life coach, I could navigate those struggles in a way that allowed me to break the self-sabotaging habits and addictions.

We often find ourselves in the struggle but are afraid to ask for help. By asking for help, that's where I was able to gain my internal strength and align with what I needed to change to overcome those obstacles. I was struggling with processing thoughts, identifying what action to take next, and how to move forward.

Hiring a coach allowed me to drop the fear of running the show and move into a clear and hopeful version of my success.

Coaching Tip #2: *Don't let your emotions run the show.*

Uncontrolled emotions will bring your energy level to low vibration. Your goal is to shift to a higher vibration so the energy can move you from stuck to unstoppable. Shift the energy through movement. Do something that physically makes you move. Dancing, singing, exercising, or cleaning out a closet. Do something physical to release the stuck energy.

Then grab a journal and write out your appreciation and gratitude for the things that bring you joy and happiness.

Releasing can feel uncomfortable, but staying in those lower emotional vibrations isn't your highest and best interest. Like Taylor Swift says, "shake it off"!

A client of mine has a product-based business, where she manufactures in her home. She struggled with knowing how to expand her business in sales because her house wasn't big enough to support the growth.

When we met for coffee, she expressed her concerns and couldn't see a clear vision past her current situation and circumstance.

Shifting her belief that everything is working out for her highest and best interest required her to let go of the "how's" and focus on taking action instead.

She saw the value in hiring me as her coach so she could be supported and move past the discomfort of growing and aligning with the path to scale her business.

When the student is ready, the teacher appears.

The struggle she had was real. She had much work that she

had done to create a profitable business. Still, her passion for continually growing would require expansion. She allowed fear to creep in, causing her to think that she wouldn't be good enough or couldn't sustain growing the business and all the other reasons she shouldn't move forward.

As we began to dive deep into those concerns, she recognized that those were just thoughts, and thoughts can be changed.

She soon started seeing the vision more clearly, set solid intentions, showed up for support, and got out of her own way.

She now is outside of her home in a more extensive manufacturing facility and reaching those income levels of just shy of a quarter of million sales per year; something she didn't believe was possible when we first met. The vision she saw for her business is now her reality.

Do you see this in your story? Along the way, you may struggle to manage your frustration and indecisiveness and find the confidence and excitement for your business to grow.

Let's check-in for a moment. After reading the story above, are you ready to grow your business with confidence and excitement? Then you are prepared to talk about having consistent accountability.

I believe that consistent accountability is supported and managed by a mentor and coach. I've been on the training ground of business and life for decades, and here's the thing, I had no leadership or mentor for the longest time. I attempted to do all of this independently and wrestled with the unknowns.

Don't you hate it when you have big expectations, and they fall flat? Time and time again, you are trying new things to grow your business. You are launching new programs, offers, or promotions hoping to get that 10X but hearing crickets.

You watch other people's success and wonder how they have it, and you don't.

You second-guess what you are doing and wonder if you are smart enough to scale your business to the next level.

Spoiler alert! Those thoughts are standing in your own way to growing your business and success.

Once I realized the value of having a coach, I've had one ever since. I now hire coaches based on the needs of my business and my life. I let my ego go and stepped into my openness to receive support and guidance so I could build and maintain a successful business. My most considerable awareness was that learning to set up processes, procedures, and strategies as a business owner is valuable when looking to scale.

In addition to the foundational piece of business, I also understood the law of attraction, where like attracts like.

One of my first coaches authored a program and book, *Action Attraction* and recommended I watch the movie *The Secret*. Both created a significant turning point in my business and my life. The law of attraction focuses on like attracts like, and your thoughts have the power to manifest in your life.

When I looked back at my life, I saw that I had achieved almost everything I desired in some form or another. However, as I got older, I lost that focus and let my energy drop and I focused on what I didn't want. I realized I had stopped thinking and talking positively about business and life and replaced it with negativity.

When I connected the dots about taking negative and how it leads to more negative, I knew I needed to flip my script and start speaking differently. This awareness led to conscious language; this one area I love to support my clients in: teaching the habit of speaking positively.

At first, I wasn't sure how this would fit into my work until I discovered that it is choosing a positive thought over a negative thought and knowing the difference.

My upbringing was a struggle for me to be positive; even though I was, I had to overcome negative pushback or conversations such as:

- Too good to be true!
- The other shoe will drop.
- Who do you think you are?
- That is impossible!
- Stop thinking you can, you can't!

It wasn't easy, and if you listen to most people, you can find that their conscious language is more of a negative vibration than a positive one.

And it doesn't help being inundated with the negative focus we see in the news or being around those who won't let go of sharing how hopeless they are about business and life.

Let it all go right here, right now! This doesn't serve you professionally or personally!

If you're willing to take time to hear what you're saying and use language that moves toward a positive direction, over time, it becomes second nature. Much like working a muscle, it gets stronger. Stop magnifying the problem with your thoughts and conversations. That is what's blocking your ability to expand and grow. You can flip the script and focus on the solution whenever you want to get unstuck. When you are ready to shift and align with the solution and get out of your way, start by showing up with accountability and ongoing support. It's not too late to learn from your past.

Early in the golf course business we owned and operated, I made what I see now as a possible million-dollar mistake. The general manager invited me to learn all I could about running a golf course. My ego got in the way, and I said, "I'm good," and didn't accept the offer.

When I hired my first coach, I soon realized how I would have benefited from having taken that time to learn from the manager and how it would have put me years ahead in a shorter time frame. I learned that the support of a coach offers you not only guidance but also how they see past your blind spots. That is priceless.

Coaching Tip #3: *I believe everyone needs a guide.*

Investing in the right coach for support that you need will make all the difference – it is the best value for getting unbiased feedback and allows for accountability. You are no longer hiding out and staying stuck. Hiring a coach who can listen and offer constructive feedback can catapult your results. You don't have to do this alone.

Creating systems and practices to get laser-focused and motivated so you will keep showing up will allow you to gain momentum with clear direction.

What happens when you don't get the results you want or desire? Believe me, when I say I thought things would be more profitable by hiring someone to do the work for me. I learned that I was investing money but not getting the results. My thoughts had me thinking, "What's wrong with them?" to not be able to create my success!

Yes, I was trying to buy my way to success. I complained and spoke poorly about how others let me down and didn't fulfill my needs for my business. Based on the law of attraction, like attracts like, I kept getting the same results with each person I hired. That stopped when I discovered a phrase that I use and share with my clients to this day: "up until now." These three words allowed me to shift my thinking from the old patterns and story to create a new intention and outcome.

I knew I needed to be the C.E.O. of my business and understand my business better.

So, I got out of my way and sat on my butt, allowing for the clarity of the action I needed to take, which didn't include hiring someone. It was me knowing inside what action to take. I began to work on the business, setting up my systems and practices and hiring the best coaches to hold me accountable. The support and focus allowed me to expand my efforts and grow my profits exponentially.

Coaching Tip #4: *Keeping an evidence journal.*

Documenting what you've accomplished daily will allow you to SEE results and spark motivation. We sometimes forget all the goodness because we only focus on what's not working. Begin each night before bed with three things you accomplished, are grateful for, or what things are getting results.

The more evidence you see working in your favor, the more you will believe you can successfully scale your business!

Lessons on the Golf Course

As I learned more about the law of attraction, I began to see how women struggled to learn to play golf at the golf course. I observed them on the course while teaching them, and their true colors came out.

They treated that little white ball like they treated themselves or others; which wasn't always pleasant. When they got in the weeds or out of bounds, they couldn't see outside the current situation, so they felt defeated before they got a good look at the position of the ball. Much like in life, we feel like we are deeply entrenched in the weeds but if you only turned around, you'd see a better view and a way out.

From this discovery, I published my first book, 5 Steps to Your Own D.R.I.V.E This book focuses on how setting intentions and using the law of attraction will create better opportunities for success in your life, no longer settling for less.

Coaching Tip #5: *The "V" in D.R.I.V.E. focuses on visualizing the outcome. Daydream like a child. And do that several times a day!*

Remember, you can't get there from here. A growth mindset comes from aligning your energy with your feelings and emotions with the vision of who you will become as you show up and do the work. The difference between successful people and those who failed is that successful people didn't give up. Go in and trust that the law of attraction is always working on your behalf.

You will soon find you can connect the dots looking back and continue to scale your business with ease and flow, especially when you believe you are worth it. You. Are. Enough.

Once I shifted my thoughts and took inspired action, my business grew. As time passes and I continue to look back, I see where I level up each decade in my professional life and my mind, body, and spirit connection.

I am a lifelong learner, and I enjoy working on myself. Since I was ten years old, the drive inside began with me selling stationery and gift wrap to farmer's wives in the country so that I could get mine for free.

Now, I help others like you multiply your business's growth, climb to the next level, leave that nine to five, and reach six-figure incomes.

Isn't it time you get clear, make things happen, and go after what you want to make your business successful?

Isn't it time you have a profitable business and learn the strategies to be successful and happy?

Book a call to get started. Together we will talk about your business challenges. If we are a good fit to work together, I'll create a customized support strategy so you can kick overwhelm to the curb. **You deserve a balanced life and a thriving business as a confident and profitable business owner.**

You deserve to live your best life now!

P.S. on Branding Your Business

In 2020, I rebranded my company. My logo now consists of a butterfly but, if you look closely, the butterfly's body is a lighthouse. These are two significant symbols that play a big part in my life and how I was able to get beyond my "stuck-story" of not being able to be successful. I no longer have that impostor syndrome. I have clarity about who I am and what I have to offer to others.

My new awareness came when I realized how the lighthouse foundation built in the bedrock has a solid and sustainable structure. If built on sand, it will never hold steady and won't stand tall enough to shine its light out into the world for those who are in need and desperately need to find it.

The butterfly has the significance of transformation. We are always moving through transformational moments. The caterpillar has no idea that it will go into the cocoon and must struggle to come out on the other side as this unique and one-of-a-kind beautiful butterfly.

My logo represents the framework on one side, and another multicolor side represents the outcome of our souls' desires.

Isn't it time:

- to learn how to build your lighthouse in the bedrock and not on sand?
- to develop a framework that will allow you to explore your business?
- to create the money-making opportunities that you never dreamed could be possible "up until now?"

Ask for help so you can shine!

Let's alleviate your stress and arm you with the confidence to succeed in life and leadership.

If you only take one thing away from my story, know that you DO deserve to have a profitable business and live your best life! As Zig Ziglar would say, "Then I'll see you at the top!"

Melissa Kirkpatrick

Melissa's love for learning and confidence in teaching inspired her to expand her horizons in ways she never imagined. Every decade, she has leveled up in business and her life.

At the age of thirty, she enrolled in college to fulfill a passion for becoming a teacher while working full time and raising a family.

In her forties, after leaving teaching to pursue an opportunity of owning and operating two public golf courses full time, she taught herself to play golf. She developed a passion for coordinating women's golf sessions, liking lessons on and off the course with a program called Find Your Own D.R.I.V.E.

Behind the scenes, though, the stress of owning a family-run business became too much, and she developed habits of addiction to alcohol, overeating, and spending. The need to numb out was her coping mechanism for success and uncertainty. Being called out about her actions and integrity, Melissa didn't recognize herself, and she wasn't living what she was teaching. The desire to overcome the struggle was real, and she found a coach to support her on the journey back to herself.

Now in her fifties, after selling the courses, she launched what she realized is her true calling – a culmination of all her personal and professional experiences – a Business & Life Coaching service. Melissa's journey of learning how to overcome obstacles and push for success allows her to step up as a leader and role model now boldly, teaching others to do the same. As a sought-after motivational and transformational Business & Life Coach, Melissa speaks to organizations, virtual summits, and podcasts and works with clients individually and in groups.

She thrives upon the success of those she works with and prides herself in helping them scale their business and life from the inside out, using techniques and modalities to develop a framework utilizing techniques to build a solid foundation by overcoming their past and building for the future. Her unique style of holding others accountable and motivated has led to clients reaching their full potential and income goals with confidence and pride.

Melissa has been published in several collaboration books and is the author of the impactful self-help book 5 *Steps to Your Own D.R.I.V.E.* For two consecutive years, Melissa received the award for Life Coach BEST IN CHIC – Reader's

Choice 2021 and 2022. Now in her third year, she writes a weekly column of motivation and inspiration for The Chic Guide Cincinnati, a lifestyle publication for women in Greater Cincinnati.

Melissa is married to her high school sweetheart and has two adult sons, a granddaughter, and a grandson coming soon.

Connect with Melissa:

linkedin.com/in/melissakirkpatrick

5.

Better Business

Alex Toth | Marketing Manager and Employee Owner at Ingage Partners

Growing up, I would sit in front of the TV just for the commercials. I always wanted the latest and greatest toy. I remember begging my parents for a RipStik. The kids in the commercials just looked like they were having SO much fun and I just had to be a part of it. Years later I learned why I was so fascinated with these commercials.

Plain and simple: it was marketing. There was some genius behind the commercials that knew exactly who their audience was, what they would identify with and what they liked to do. I was their persona. So, that's why I studied Marketing in school. I wanted to connect with customers, understand them, and bring something into their lives to bring them joy.

While working towards my degree in marketing, I also started to understand more about the complexities of economy, climate change, poverty, and racial injustices. I became passionate about helping and not hurting. I wanted to be a part of real change, and avoid giving handouts but rather a hand up. I wanted to learn how to do more than just recycle. I wanted to actually support underrepresented groups, rather than simply adding a frame to my profile picture on Facebook. My eyes were opened to a world of pain and suffering. The stories that I witnessed are not mine to share but what I can share with you is a common theme of injustice. I witnessed people hurting and this privileged white girl wept. I wept at the injustices that I was blind to for so many years. I wept because it wasn't fair.

"Well, life isn't fair." That's what they say, right? Sure, if I'm a kid throwing a fit because I wanted the orange popsicle and got the purple, you can tell me that. But you can't tell me that it's fair that the color of my skin grants me certain privileges. You can't tell me that it's fair I don't have to worry about going hungry when millions around the world do. And you can't tell me that it's fair that certain communities are disproportionately harmed by the climate crisis. Because it isn't. It isn't fair.

Full of conviction, I asked myself, "What can I do?" I had to be part of the solution.

I started to realize RipStiks weren't what people needed. The more I looked at my options upon graduation, the less motivated I was to work for a company that was not helping people or the planet, but actually the opposite. I never lost sight of my mission to bring joy to people through the vehicle of marketing, but I didn't know how to blend these passions into a career.

Upon graduation, it seemed I had only two options. I could apply to corporations, climb the corporate ladder, and make my way in the marketing world for a decent paycheck. Or, I could swap a large paycheck for purpose and go the non-profit route helping people in need; perhaps still in a marketing capacity. I chose the latter.

I started by joining AmeriCorps and worked locally to support poverty initiatives in Cincinnati. Then, I moved to Mexico to care for vulnerable children and families teaching English and hosting mission trip teams. At that time, I believed the only way to fulfill my calling was to do this kind of work. During those times I witnessed incredible stories of life-change and I got to be a part of it – what a privilege! I wouldn't change my experiences for anything in the world; and fully and wholeheartedly believe nonprofits are doing incredible work. But, in the end, I got burnt out and I wasn't growing as a marketing professional. Being a badass Marketer was still on the agenda.

So now what? Try the corporate route and help non-profits financially through donations? Perhaps. Nonprofits need money so maybe I could make a difference this way. For me, I needed something more. I wanted to go to work every day knowing that my efforts were contributing to a greater good. And that's when I learned about Certified B Corps.

Transitioning home due to the pandemic, I was looking for what was next. I remember being at my in-laws and receiving a text from a former boss that said, "Where are you? Are you in Cincinnati or Mexico? Anne has a company, Ingage, who is looking for someone to work in marketing." At the time of my interview, (like a good candidate...) I didn't know much about the company. I just knew it was marketing and I needed a job, so this wasn't the time to be picky. I remember being on a call with the CEO as part of the interview process and she asked me if I was familiar with Certified B Corporations (B Corps). I said no (like a good candidate...) and she explained that it is a certification businesses get that holds them accountable to meeting certain social and environmental standards. They care not only about being profitable but equally about their impact on people and the planet. A triple bottom line. This was exactly what I was looking for.

The B Corp community is on a mission to transform the way business is done and have a measurable impact. Without the certification, there is no standard of accountability or transparency. It is overwhelming to discern if a company that says they "do good" *actually* does good. There are multiple definitions for different types of social enterprises and its complex to understand how each entity measures their impact. Below is an image outlining the different types of social enterprises. As for how they measure their impact, that requires looking individually at how each entity operates.

Again, is this bad? No, but it is certainly confusing. As a consumer and someone looking for meaningful employment, it's a lot to navigate.

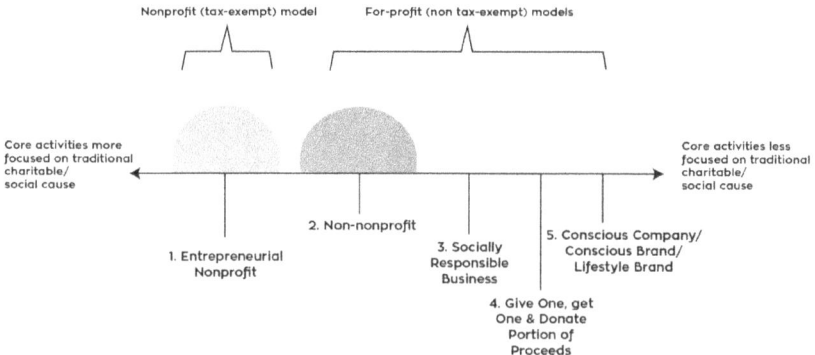

1

The B Corp Certification serves to bring clarity to the chaos. I know that I can trust the brands that carry that logo. I know that when I "see the B," the company pays their employees a livable wage and provides holistic benefits, has consciously evaluated the environmental impact of their efforts, is/are actively fighting climate change, and is invested in making a difference in their communities and beyond. I can tell you with 100% confidence that B Corps are indeed a legitimate way to discern a company that actually does good v.s. a company that just says they do good.

To become certified, organizations start by taking the B Impact Assessment. This is the most credible tool a company can use to measure its impact on its workers, community, environment, and customers. Companies answer questions in five areas and are scored accordingly. If their scores are high enough, they'll receive the certification.

The areas of evaluation are as follows:

- **Governance**: evaluates a company's overall mission, engagement around its social/environmental impact, ethics, and transparency. This section also evaluates the ability of a company to protect their mission and formally consider stakeholders in decision making through their corporate structure (e.g. benefit corporation) or corporate governing documents.
- **Workers**: evaluates a company's contributions to its employees' financial security, health and safety, wellness, career development, and engagement and satisfaction. In addition, this section recognizes business models designed to benefit workers, such as companies that are at least 40% owned by non-executive employees and those that have workforce development programs to support individuals with barriers to employment.
- **Community**: evaluates a company's engagement with and impact on the communities in which it operates, hires from, and sources from. Topics include diversity, equity and inclusion, economic impact, civic engagement, charitable giving, and supply chain management. In addition, this section recognizes business models that are designed to address specific community-oriented problems, such as poverty alleviation through fair trade sourcing or distribution via microenterprises, producer cooperative models, locally-focused economic development, and formal charitable giving commitments.
- **Environment**: evaluates a company's overall

environmental management practices as well as its impact on the air, climate, water, land, and biodiversity. This includes the direct impact of a company's operations and, when applicable, its supply chain and distribution channels. This section also recognizes companies with environmentally innovative production processes and those that sell products or services that have a positive environmental impact. Some examples might include products and services that create renewable energy, reduce consumption or waste, conserve land or wildlife, provide less toxic alternatives to the market, or educate people about environmental problems.

- **Customers**: evaluates a company's stewardship of its customers through the quality of its products and services, ethical marketing, data privacy and security, and feedback channels. In addition, this section recognizes products or services that are designed to address a particular social problem for or through its customers, such as health or educational products, arts and media products, serving underserved customers/clients, and services that improve the social impact of other businesses or organizations.[2]

Scoring high in these categories can manifest in a lot of different ways. For us at Ingage Partners, a Certified B Corp and IT and Business Consulting company, we were created out of the idea to do business differently and eleven years later, you can see it daily around the organization. Our Slack channel is flooded with people donating blood, planting trees, sharing volunteer opportunities, and advocating for a myriad of causes.

Beyond it "just being part of our culture," one way we live our B Corp values is by being an Employee Owned business. Simply put, when the company wins, we all win. Profit sharing places an emphasis on our collective interest and fosters an inclusive community that extends to our families, clients, and communities.

We also have a Green Team that keeps us honest in reaching our environmental goals. They educate, inspire, and enable Ingage employee (Ingagers) to promote environmental sustainability at Ingage and within our homes and communities. They create a culture of sustainability by engaging employees to make small, consistent habit changes that will lead to substantial impact over time. Most recently, this looked like figuring out a sustainable coffee solution moving away from one-time use K-Cups and implementing a zero-waste solution.

I could go on and on but I'll leave you with just a couple more ideas that may spark something for you or your business. When I first started, there was an emphasis on volunteering but I thought that was just for the one day a year that we set aside as an Ingage Holiday to give back. While that one day is great and leads to a whole lot of fun and impact, everyone on the team is involved in their communities beyond what we have called "Pay it Forward Day." Ingagers get forty-eight hours of paid volunteer time to invest in our communities. This allows me to stay connected with the organizations I know and love. I literally spent my birthday this year planting trees and got paid for it!

Our diversity, equity, and inclusion efforts are also ongoing. In today's climate, it is more important than ever that brands recognize the opportunities they have with their platforms. Opportunities to advocate for what is fair and just and to bring awareness to the challenges our society is facing. Beyond just reaching people on our platforms, we make space to learn, grow, and have honest conversations around topics like how we expand economic opportunities for people of color and support underrepresented communities.

One way that we are addressing underrepresented individuals is through our Thrive Accelerator program. Tech boot camps are great for quickly teaching individuals how to code, test, etc. but then what? They need a job with a mentor that can fill in the gaps that they haven't had the time to learn in a twelve to fifteen-week course. That's where we come in; we provide the necessary mentoring for individuals to truly make an impact in the tech industry. Since 2016, we've seen over a hundred individuals increase their annual compensation by 5X. That is a tangible change. That is better business.

So, am I solving world hunger, the climate crisis, or eliminating racism like I set out to do? Well, not exactly. But, I'd argue that every day someone on our team is making strides towards a better tomorrow. And, I am working somewhere that values people and the planet as much as they value being a successful business.

Yes, a successful business. I know you may be thinking this all sounds fine and dandy but I'm not even profitable yet. To you I say: just take the Impact Assessment. The tool will help you think upfront as you set the foundation for your business and help mold your DNA. Should you achieve a Certified B Corporation status, you will gain credibility as a company. People will want to work *for* and *with* you and people will want to buy *from* you. Not to mention the community of like-minded individuals and businesses you will meet along the way!

I've just scratched the surface of what we are doing, and our friends in the B Corp community have different programs in place to achieve their B Corp status. It looks different for every business, every work culture. What remains the same is our passion to serve our neighbors, love our planet, and use business as a force for good. My intention in sharing all this with you is simply to bring awareness to an option you may not have known about. And perhaps inspire you to join the movement to do business, better. If nothing else, consider "looking for the B" next time you make a purchasing decision because I believe together, we can make a difference.

Notes

1. Company, Conscious. "A Look inside the 6 Types of Social Enterprises." Medium, B The Change, 17 Feb. 2022, https://bthechange.com/a-look-inside-the-6-types-of-social-enterprises-fd51331d47de.

2. https://www.bcorporation.net/en-us/

Alex Toth

Alex Toth is the Marketing Manager at Ingage Partners, a Purpose-Driven Technology and Business consulting company.

From website creation, podcast producing, and SEO, she's dabbled in it all. Alex most enjoys creative projects involving design and storytelling. She's played a key role in creating documentaries and regularly produces video content. She has also planned many events, mostly in the non-profit space.

Her eyes were opened to the pain and suffering of the world in 2012 and has since been on a mission to be a catalyst of change in her community and beyond. Throughout her career, this has manifested in different ways; most recently advocating for businesses to become Certified B Corporations. Alex believes that, together, we can transform the way business is done and our world will be better for it.

Outside of her professional life, you'll likely find her outdoors or spending time with her dog.

Connect with Alex:

https://www.linkedin.com/in/alex-toth-31189866/

6.

Aspire to Inspire

Jaime Lyons | Co-Founder ASMI LLC

There comes a time in most people's lives that they wish they had a life that was true to themselves. A life that uses their talents, wisdom, and passion and fulfills a missing piece of life's puzzle. I have had the revelation that I wanted to do good in the world while owning my own business. This was a direction of my own choice. I wanted to make my own time for what I wanted and feel the satisfaction of making my business grow and flourish. Obstacles and challenges happen along the way as with anything in life, but the greatest and scariest thing is to own a business, especially in times of uncertainty like we have seen with recent years. I, like others, have been asked "When are you going to get a "real" job? It's a question that bites to the core and makes one question their journey. The truth about most women in business is that we are good at it. Once we have our minds set on something, we meticulously turn a dream into reality and for good measure, make it the best there can be. Look at women like media mogul Oprah Winfrey, Sara Blakely of Spanx, and Tory Burch of Tory Burch clothing and fashion. These are women who have made names for themselves and taken their success and used it to help other female entrepreneurs. Women have the ability if they have the drive. **A woman who can apply the who, what, when, where, and why to herself and act towards the promise of mothering a business is a success story worth telling.**

Who? It is said that devilish women are a bother and good ones are a bore, but what of the good women who devilishly leap from the mundane and pursue a path of uncertainty and promise as business owners? Why are some women more at ease with business ownership and can take charge of their lives with the uncertainty of business? These are women who revolutionized the world facing adversity and fear of the unknown and charge forward to make dreams into reality. No businesswoman is an island. When you launch your own business, you will have to do every job from accounting to production. There are some jobs that you will have no idea how to do, and you will need to research and ask professionals for insight and help. Growing a business will grow you into a fearless and more knowledgeable woman. Fight the temptation to do everything alone. There are so many other women that are willing and eager to help others succeed and lead you to wiser business decisions. Find local networking groups such as BNI, local chamber of commerce, or your local small business administration office for details on who to know groups to help you grow your business. If you have a supportive community to lean on, you will be empowered to take larger smarter risks.

Fast Fact: Only one in three businesses in the world are owned by women, according to World Bank [1]

What? Every leap starts with a first step. It takes a leap of faith in yourself to begin a business, to move against the current and all that is familiar and comfortable like a real job with steady hours and a regular paycheck. So, why do it? Why not get a "real" job and feel comfortable and unburdened? Owning a business allows you to steer your own career and create hours to enable success in a market where women are only making 79% of what their male counterparts earn[2]. The question of what drives a woman to make the leap of faith in herself in a world where the struggle for equality is still real and the fight for becoming more than a gender is prevalent in all areas of the world. Most business women start out as dreamers. They are dreamers that take an idea and transform it into something of substance.

First steps start with dreams of what we can do, dreams of what it would be like if we could apply our talents in ourselves instead of a big corporation that doesn't value those talents or the woman that has them. Maybe someone told you that you should create a business from your talent, and you should go for it. It can start with the difficulty reentering the workforce after having a child or caring for a relative. The reasons are endless and should only matter to *you* and what drives *you*. It gets you thinking and dreaming. This is an exciting first step that many begin on their path but don't move past. Dreams are where you create a world of ideas and of what can be. A place with no restrictions and no realities that bog down the thoughts that flow. Dreams are easy, they are vivid and endless, but it takes more than dreaming; it takes action.

When? When do we take a dream and turn it into a plan of action that transforms a possibility into a reality? This is that part of business that can be fun to some and to others it is a little more tedious. A quote that resonated with me through this process was from Jim Rohn: "We must all suffer from one of two pains: the pain of discipline or the pain of regret. The difference is discipline weighs ounces while regret weighs tons." The hard work you put into yourself, and your business is the work that will lead you to success. This is where aspiring business owners must research and plan. What investment do you need to have to get started? What location? Can it be fully online, or do you need storefronts? How do you financially support yourself and family while your business is growing and not providing the comfort that a "real" job can give? Don't let these questions discourage you. They are the real and hard questions you need to ask yourself. This is the nitty gritty part that can be hard to navigate, but thankfully there are resources that can be found that help with these questions you will have and there will be many. These resources can also help provide answers and solutions. So, don't shy away from them. Remember life is a marathon, not a sprint.

Where? Where do you start? All questions are important in creating your business, but this can seem like the most difficult. You have dreamt up the next successful female-owned business and you have planned it out with a product or service, a budget you researched you will probably need, and all the details that you think will help get you to the start of making your business. This is the phase where the actual work starts like with painting a room. I always say it's 90% prep work before the real work begins. This is that phase where all the prep work comes together to get things started. This is also the phase you take to understand your market. What is available in your area that is similar to what you want to do? Research those businesses. Women and local businesses are open to sharing ideas and building each other up. I promise. Reach out. Aspire to Inspire. You finally can register that name that is available that you feel is the heart and soul of the company and you can open your bank account, start up the website and get everything to make your dreams a reality. My suggestion in this phase is to focus on progress instead of perfection. It will foster a culture prioritizing a growth mindset and allow room for creativity and new strategies. Remember this is your business that you are growing and much like mothering a child, you are mothering your business into innovation and growth.

Why? Essentially the most important question to ask yourself is "Why?" Why do you want to own a business? It's a question that starts everything on your path. It is the question that can make you take the leap of faith from quitting a career and doing everything on your own. Every woman has their own reasons to begin a business. Many I know have started after starting their family. They quit working in the corporate world and began their family. After years of being out of the workforce, it is more difficult to re-enter, and they found that the opportunities weren't available to them like they used to. Left with fewer options, and a desire to be independent and thrive in a world that has more meetings than playdates. This happened to me, and I know it has for so many others. I think mothers that have made this decision have bigger priorities for their families and the freedom of time they can have for their family's needs.

Running a business can be stressful as well as rewarding. Self-care is just as important in the long run. Owning a business is not for the timid or faint of heart. It takes bravery and support from others to help with its success. Women in leadership roles like business ownership are some of the bravest creative risk takers I have ever met. There are times in business ownership that you will be faced with challenges that require your decision and creativity to succeed and conquer. Thinking outside of the box, accepting change, and constantly researching to keep up with the changing market will take you far in business ownership. I want to encourage whoever is reading this that you can change your fate and your career if you take the leap.

Owning your own business is a way to make your own rules and create your own path for success. Each woman's path is different; and, at the end of the day, if you work towards your personal goals, you are achieving *your own success story*. Define yourself and your methods and don't be afraid to ask for help from others along the way. Above all the recommendations and advice you may take from this, learn to say "NO." I will be the first to admit that I'm still working on this. This is part of your self-care and responsibility to yourself. It is okay to say "no," yes, even to clients or customers. You can create your own boundaries in your business to allow you more time to focus on what you want to do to succeed. I was once told by another business colleague that you want to run your business, rather than let your business run you. It is easy to get caught up in everything your business needs and let it consume your time and effort. Make time for yourself in all of it and you, your family, and your business will thrive.

I started both of my companies with many questions and uncertain of the direction to take to find answers. Much like a parent, I was new and naïve to how to get the information for starting a business and its development. Thankfully, the internet and local resources like your local chamber of commerce and local business network groups can help guide you. My first business was a lot of researching, scrambling, and a whole bunch of creativity for reasons of finance and excitement. Both companies are different in each way; much like individuals are. One is more established and refined, made with purpose and driven by love, beauty, and altruism. The other is still young, easy-going, and quirky. They began with the dreams and thoughts of what I wanted at the time of their inception, and what I could do with my talents. One of the greatest things about owning a business is the ability to create and do what you love and are passionate about. My journey began much like the essential questions to ask and was one that was my own journey. It was never a planned moment, more of a "right place and time" and having the right conversation with the right person. ASMI was born in a moment of conversation.

ASMI began in 2018 as a conversation between two women from a local garden club. We appreciated what each other could bring to the table and wanted to make a difference in others' lives. My business partner is from India and told of the hardships many women in her community faced. I was a community volunteer that created social events and included charities to fundraise for at these events. With these key ingredients, we brainstormed ideas for a business. ASMI was born. The word stands for "self-respect" in Sanskrit and the company is based on beauty and benevolence. We provide fine silver jewelry and handmade accessories from India that support organizations and groups that help women and communities. ASMI strongly believes in the sustainability of fair trade and traditional handmade craft and its importance to our future civilization and provides ethically sourced fine fashion jewelry and accessories for a market of altruistic and up-on-trend people, our shop/site is the answer; for the altruistic Greater Cincinnati consumer market – and beyond. We dedicate ourselves to thoughtful sourcing of meaningful goods that are ethical and sustainable unlike other retail and jewelry retail in the area that do not disclose where their products are procured. Ethical fashion is an umbrella term for fair-trade and covers a range of issues such as working conditions, exploitation, sustainable products, and human welfare. We are part of a sustainable fashion movement fostering change towards greater ecological integrity and social justice. We have found as we've grown that uniquely designed, fine jewelry is a passion of ours. We create and procure pieces that have meaning and beauty while being created by organizations that help others that support our motto of Beauty & Benevolence.

BEAUTY AND BENEVOLENCE

ASMI

FAIRTRADE HANDMADE
ACCESSORIES & FINE
SILVER JEWELRY

WWW.ASMISTYLE.COM
FOLLOW US: FB @ASMISTYLE
INSTA ASMI.STYLE

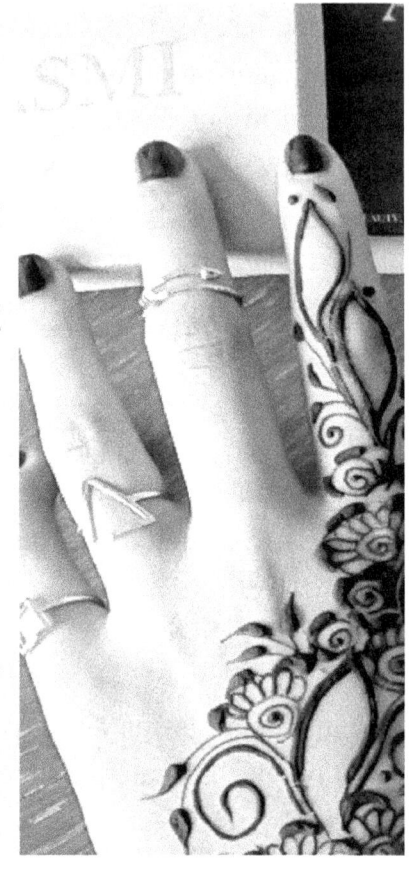

ASMI is becoming the business that I am proud to have co-founded. It is the kind of business that has deep meaning to me, but has also begun to receive accolades since 2021. ASMI won the Duke Energy Small Business Grant for women and minority owned businesses. We were published in the NKY Chamber of Commerce magazine, featured in many online blogs, pages, and groups online. ASMI was featured in a Podcast for Her Journey in October 2020. I was featured as December 2020 Northern Kentucky Leading Ladies for my efforts in business with ASMI and recently featured in an article for Voyage Ohio in 2021. From winning the Northern

Kentucky Chamber Business Impact award to being a finalist in 2021 and 2022 Best of Northern Kentucky Jeweler and Cincinnati Best of the Best Women Owned Business and Jeweler. A couple of ASMI jewelry pieces I have designed have been featured in *Creative Reflections*, a book that showcases women and their creative talents. I am proud of the business not only through the hard work to get it to where it is, but as a child watching it grow and succeed. Don't get me wrong, there are plenty of obstacles in the way of growth.

The pandemic of 2020 was especially difficult for retail businesses, and we had to put our thinking caps on to ride the tide and make it through. Uncertainty is the medium for creativity. Creativity thrived, either by necessity or lack of the normal business of day-to-day business. This moment in time really taught me that perseverance and dedication can make anything possible while thinking outside of the box was absolutely necessary. This was the beginning of ASMI's momentum and where we started on designing some of our original jewelry pieces that new collections are created each year because of a moment that could have been disastrous, we created anew. Local businesses banded together as a community to help each other, and it was one of the most beautiful moments of camaraderie I've ever experienced. Business leaders worked together and brainstormed many creative ideas for each other during this time. I always look for a silver lining in every moment, and I really think that this is the good that was made during this trying time in my, and all of our, journey. A testament to strong women and to a few of the ladies working on this book is that we were pulled together during the pandemic by creative, aspiring women working together, making new connections and possibilities for one another to inspire growth. Pulling through certain moments and reveling in others is part of the excitement of business ownership.

Moments of inspiration can occur at the strangest of times. While working with my business partner one day in Summer of 2021 at ASMI, we once again threw around some ideas for a new business. This time it was on a more lighthearted fun side. Why not start a dropship business? Drop shipping is a supply chain management method in which retailers do not keep goods in stock but instead transfer customer's orders to a manufacturer that ships the goods directly to the customer. This is a business where we design all the fun carefree things people get to express the less serious side of themselves. With a range of accessories from fun t-shirts to funny dog collar IDs, it's a business that we can wind down and have fun with. Tru Story was born in late summer of 2021 and is still a baby with much more to grow into.

It was much simpler to start since we already had a grasp for starting one and where to go. With that and the fun approach to what kind of business it is, we enjoyed starting it and its persona is very lighthearted. I enjoy creating designs with fun in mind. Starting a second business after the first one is only a few years old and went through a major pandemic that rocked the retail world may seem like an insane decision. People will say "there is never a right time to start a business," and that "you just have to make time." This decision was based partly on having fun and carefree merchandise, but with drop shipping, it takes much of the on-hand work from us and allows us to focus on the creativity side of the business.

> "Life is a journey, not a destination" – Ralph Waldo Emerson.

What is your journey? Who, what, when, where, and why has it begun and where will it take you? This is one of my favorite quotes. One that I have in one of my new pendant designs for ASMI, actually. It makes me look at life and my business as growth and progress that will take me to another phase or place in my life that will likely take me on another journey to something else. My business journey has changed me in positive ways that I never knew about myself and that I never thought possible. I am stronger and more empowered than when I started and I am working on improving myself and my businesses every single day. Take time to improve yourself and make your life your own. Reflect on where you are now, where you are going, and where you have been and congratulate yourself on your journey. Aspire to become your best you and enjoy where it takes you.

Notes

1. "World Bank Blogs: Women Entrepreneurs Needed: Stat!" World Bank Blogs, 5 Mar. 2020, https://blogs.worldbank.org/.
2. Li, Yun. "CNBC." NBC, 16 Apr. 2019, https://www.nbc.com/networks/cnbc.

Jaime Lyons

Jaime resides in Union, KY with an exceptional family of mostly men. Co-owner of Asmi and Tru Story, she and her businesses have received many accolades and awards. Author and women's advocate, she incorporates beauty and benevolence into her businesses.

Jaime began her relationship with fashion through her rebellion of school uniforms in the audience of the occasional nun or priest. She attended University of Cincinnati, where she majored in Biology and journeyed into business entrepreneurship.

Connect with Jaime:
linkedin.com/in/jaime-lyons-1953a843

7.

Reluctant Entrepreneur

Kim Vollbrecht | Pipeline Plumber, President of V2 Strategies

3 Signs It's Time to Take the Leap!

I was coming up on ten weeks pregnant with twins – a single mom by choice – sitting in my parish priest's office.

I had barely started explaining my situation to my pastor when he interrupted me, saying:

"Kim – I have only one question."

I took a breath, nodded and said, "Okay."

And he replied: "How can we help?"

I struggle to put in words the power behind that simple question. Reflecting on my Catholic upbringing and education, I had prepared myself for a catechetical conversation. Instead, I was offered a continuing welcome from a community that had already accepted me.

At that moment, I stopped second-guessing my choices. I walked out of the parish center with renewed confidence in my decision to take the leap into motherhood.

I keep coming back to this vignette every time I wonder why it took me so long to realize I was born to be an entrepreneur. For the longest time, I couldn't figure out why it seemed so central. After all, it would be another ten years before I started my own company.

Now, I see it as the catalyst for redefining my purpose in life. My "why" had changed – I just hadn't realized it yet. And as my new "why" crystalized, both my "what" and "how" no longer fit. I'm an entrepreneur *and* a mom today because of the process I went through to bring my why, what, and how in sync.

I'm a midlife entrepreneur. Making the change from career employee to business owner isn't for everyone. I never thought I *could* do it, until I felt I *had* to do it. And at that point- everything fell into place. I'm not saying it was ever smooth and easy – but it just seemed to fit. And it all started with "why."

I'm sharing that journey, in the hopes it will inspire other later-in-life entrepreneurs to make that leap for themselves. I wanted to make a bigger impact, to leave my corner of the world better than I found it. And being the best mom I could be – while supporting my family – was my new purpose.

1) Your "Why" Has Changed

My "career path" spanned a range of organizations (government, corporate and not-for-profit) and functions (policy, advocacy, communications). Each move took me on a new tangent, involving new skills, new responsibilities, and new stakeholders. In each case, I convinced my new boss that I could make the transition – and the burden of proof rested solely on my shoulders. Wouldn't that make more sense as the inspiration to be my own boss?

Then it struck me: I wasn't the sole driver behind those moves. While the urge for change was internal, its realization was dependent on external opportunities. Absent the right opportunity, where I was the right fit, I had a fallback: stay in place.

In fact, I wasn't looking for a change when I decided to become a mom. That choice was born in quiet moments, when I'd reflect on my life, and think: *Is this all there is?* I wasn't sad or upset – I just felt a gap. And then I felt it: *I want to be a mom.*

I was stunned. All my life, I'd fought against "wife/mother" as a career choice. In my idyllic small-town childhood, smart girls were encouraged to become a teacher, librarian, or a nun – with the first two being a stopping place on the road to wife and mother.

That just wasn't going to be me. I rebelled against the "box" I was assigned to simply because I was a girl. I didn't know what I wanted to do – just that it wasn't one of the two options that showed up on my career aptitude tests.

I also knew, after listening to my mom's conversation with a widowed neighbor who remarried as her only means of support, that I was never going to depend on someone else for my livelihood.

The "why" that led to a fulfilling career came from proving a 'girl' could be strong, smart, and self-sufficient. She could "make it." Until the day I realized that "making it" wasn't enough.

2) Your "What" Isn't Enough

I went into motherhood thinking of it as an "and" decision. I could continue my career and be a mom. But the mindset change that led to my motherhood leap of faith was stubborn. It changed how I looked at tradeoffs I was making in all parts of my life.

I was fortunate to have multiple opportunities to sharpen and reapply my skills. I moved to new assignments, or companies, every three years. I reveled in working with new people, in new situations, and on new challenges. After each challenge was resolved, I'd got that same "there must be something more" itch.

Over time, my contributions stemmed from an "outsider" perspective. I was keen to contribute but wasn't wedded to the status quo. In effect, I was an "internal" consultant – and, frequently, a change agent. And just like the prophets in the bible, that "truth-speaking" role isn't broadly appreciated in your own "country," or company.

While I had a wonderful corporate career, with a broad range of opportunities, the work ultimately stopped feeling like "making it." In an "up and out" culture, stepping back – looking for reduced responsibility, travel, and hours – isn't really an option.

3) Your "How" Is Hiding in Plain Sight

You know the saying, "If all you have is a hammer, everything looks like a nail"?

That's only true if you're the only person who owns a tool.

An amazing thing happened when I shared my desire to be a mom with a few close friends. They immediately connected me to women they knew who were also single moms by choice. I didn't have to figure this out on my own – I could talk with experienced moms and learn from their journeys.

It's the same when you start your business. The tools you need to succeed already exist. There are other people seeking answers to the same questions.

And here's the "secret sauce": you ALREADY have most of the

skills you need to be an entrepreneur. You just need to view them in a different light.

These are the core skills I used the most as a mom that made it easier to launch my business:

<u>Planning:</u> This has never been my strength. I'm the visionary, wing-it, adapt-as-we-go-along type. I'm always focused on a goal and purpose, happy to leave the details up to others.

I spent a month before I moved forward on my journey to motherhood stopping every hour or so and asking, "How would this be different if I were a mom?" While a lot of my answers were wide of the mark, I was able to identify resources, support systems and lifestyle changes that would be critical in my shift to a working mother.

I took notes, researched options, and then repeated my "silent planning" process, until I felt I had it nailed. While of course I didn't, the preparation made it easier to adapt to each new twist and turn in a (relatively) calm and pragmatic way.

<u>Enlisting Mentors:</u> Every "how-to" resource for business owners stresses the importance of a Personal Board of Advisors. You need a mentor with experience in your area of business, business experts who can coach you on sales and finance, and others who have strengths that match your weaknesses.

My mom-to-be example was my local Mothers of Twins club. I kept my sanity, and my kids made it through their first year;

largely as a result of this group's expertise and support. I learned how to tackle common mom challenges (when will my babies sleep through the night?), and multiple-specific techniques (one bowl, one spoon for feeding; best strollers for fitting in a store aisle).

There were moms with multiple sets of twins, working moms, stay-at-home moms, older moms, and moms with special needs children. It was a no-judgment, we've-all-been-there, "Honey you're doing the best you can and that's good enough" zone.

In the same way, you can't launch a business on your own. Surround yourself with the version of these people that works for your business, and recruit your own board of advisors.

<u>Adaptability:</u> If you read point one (planning), you'd think this was my forte. But when you've got two little earthlings (or a business and employees) depending on you, options become a lot more limited. Every decision has tradeoffs – and the thing that gets traded off the most is you.

Your body's nutrients support those developing babies; despite the fact you can't listen to a food commercial without getting nauseous. Your sleep is secondary to your children's nighttime cries, feedings, and changes. Your six-month-old needs surgery, one son is diagnosed with Tourette's, the All-State Band auditions are the same day (but two hours away) as the premier local wrestling tournament. You just figure out how to make it work.

The trade-offs are worth it – it's just hard to appreciate that when you've forgotten to put on "real" shoes before heading off on your commute. There will come a time when you can reflect on all you've accomplished. You just have to get through that incubator stage first. And then the toddler one. And then the tee ball one.

Here's the secret about "stages": there will always be another one. It's true as a parent, and it's true as a business owner. So, remember to breathe. Live in the moment. Appreciate what is, and remember *why* you're doing this. And then keep moving forward.

<u>Validation</u>: This is critical. I remember calling my mom up two days after she left me alone with my newborns, sobbing and saying "I'm a horrible mom." When asked "Why ever would you say that?" I said: "All I do is feed them, change them, and give them baths." And she replied (with a note of exasperation), *"What else do you think you should do?"*

I was comparing myself to the baby magazine moms who spent hours massaging their infants, dressing them in elaborate layettes, and organizing glamor shots every month. I'd gone from being a top-ranked employee, to an exhausted ghost of myself who was thrilled when the daily laundry loads fell into the single digits.

Similarly, as business owners, we can get distracted by someone else's success story. A trusted advisor suggests a shift in our business model, or target customer, or pricing. A business that launched when yours did is wildly successful.

Suddenly, we're not measuring up. Our "should be" list grows, and anxiety sets in.

Those moments *will* happen. Here's how you can be prepared:

Stay centered on your "why." Why did you start your business? Who do you serve? How do you make their lives better? At this point, you're past the visionary stage – you have real life examples. I started V2 Strategies so I could be the mom I wanted to be. I love what I do – and even more, I'm grateful for the difference launching my business has made for my family

Appreciate your impact. Several years ago, a friend offered me a share of his newest venture. In return, he asked me to help out with his marketing. I was stunned, telling him I didn't see how I would be able to provide services for him that matched the value he was giving me. He looked me in the eye and said, "I'm not worried about that. I know you're a giver, and this is my way of letting you know that I see what you do."

You are making a difference. For your employees, your family, and your community. That difference goes beyond the balance sheet, the pay rate, and customer reviews. You're changing lives in ways big and small. If you don't know what that impact is – ask.

Live grateful. At my dad's funeral, countless people in our hometown came up to my brothers and me to say "Your dad was so proud of you." We were stunned – because he never said that to us, either in words or by his actions. We had a positive impact on his life – but he never let us know that.

It took me a while to get over being mad at him for not telling, or showing, us what he told everyone else. We all had complicated relationships with him. But now I know that wasn't his choice. He simply didn't know how to do it any differently. And I'm grateful that so many people gave me that peek into my dad's heart.

In different ways, my brothers and I have all chosen to live differently. We choose not to have our families and friends wonder whether they matter to us.

It's why I keep a gratitude journal. At the end of the day, I reflect on the unexpected joys that came my way – or the extra grace that kept me from a total meltdown. Then, I make sure I let those to whom I'm grateful know the difference they made.

Landing Where You Belong

Before she left home to go to secretarial school, my mom spent a summer in Glacier National Park. Her love of the outdoors led to two-week camping trips every summer, where she single-handedly packed, unpacked, fed, and supervised our eight-person family to and through every National Park west of the Mississippi.

She kept her growing family together as my dad completed

law school, moved several times, then settled in our small town in southern Minnesota. In her "spare time" while we were in school, she kept two law offices running, and launched tax preparation and bookkeeping businesses that she kept going into her 70s.

If you asked my mom what she did, she'd laugh and said "Oh, I'm *just* a homemaker." She'd tell you about her six kids, her fifteen grandkids, her three great-grands, her church, and her bridge club.

That's what was important to her. So, that's how I saw her.

What I didn't see was how she found a way to feed her entrepreneurial soul while having dinner on the table every night at six, making it to all of our school events, and setting up jigsaw puzzles on snowy winter nights.

When my dad couldn't cope with a particularly stressful incident and disappeared for several weeks, leaving my mom with six kids under ten and none of us had any idea of where he was, she soldiered through and never let us know that anything was wrong.

Mom was the rock that protected and nurtured her family, while keeping mom-the-entrepreneur in the background.

By trying to emulate what she gave us as a mom, I was following her example as a business owner. Mom's superpower was making order from chaos. Local farmers would walk in the door with milk crates full or receipts, orders, and checking account statements, and she'd turn them into balance sheets, tax returns, and budget plans. And when schools closed early due to weather, she automatically prepared entertainment, feeding schedules, and sleeping arrangements for the dozen kids who stayed at our house.

Where my mom turns chaos into balanced columns of numbers, I see ways to reconfigure puzzle pieces that create a new picture of success. Mom had a firm grasp on the present based on her knowledge of the past; I find pathways to a desired future that build on what already exists.

My version of my mother's gift has helped me keep my sanity as a mom – and build strong bonds with my sons. Friends and family turn to me for ideas on how to navigate out of a tough situation – or achieve a lifelong dream. Clients look for ways to connect their sales and marketing so everything runs like clockwork – and they can spend more time doing what they do well.

My "aha" moment in the parish office gave me the grace to stop second-guessing my decision, and the confidence to take more leaps of faith in all areas of my life.

Kim Vollbrecht

Kimberlee Vollbrecht is the founder and President of V2 Strategies. As the Pipeline Plumber, she helps businesses find and fix leaks in their sales pipeline. She takes a simple approach to building sales funnel systems: if it doesn't work for you, it doesn't work.

The V2 Team provides sales funnel solutions work for SMB because they're based on each company's customer journey; fit their current sales and marketing process; and support their longer term goals and objectives. Their process helps clients:

- Get more customers like their best customers
- Weed out the bad fits
- Create a compelling nurture experience, and
- Support customer loyalty and referrals

When she's not providing clients with success solutions, Kim loves time spent with her twin sons, family, and friends, and nature walks with her rescue dog Roxie. She particularly enjoys Activities that center on solving mysteries or putting puzzle pieces together. As a child, she'd start jigsaw puzzles from the inside out, creating a picture from individual pieces that naturally fit together. That ability to see connections first, and then assemble the picture, has helped her successfully build coalitions, shift opinions, and drive sales throughout her career.

Connect with Kim:

linkedin.com/in/kimvollbrecht

Conclusion

Thank you for supporting the Women in Business authors by purchasing this book. The goal of the Women in Business book series is to inspire women to thrive in life, career and business. When women thrive, society thrive, businesses thrive and families thrive. Honestly, when women thrive, the world thrives.

We are grateful to the authors for saying yes to being a part of this series. Writing a chapter can be scary and imposter syndrome can hit. But the best way to impact others is through story-telling.

While creating the Women in Business series, we invited authors to join us for a weekend retreat, Overnight Author, to connect and start their writing journey. On the second day, we had five women hanging out a co-working space chatting about their life experiences and how to include them in their chapter. While a woman was sharing her story, other women were nodding their head in agreement. We all had similar stories and could truly relate to each other. At the end of the day, we all felt closer to each other. A tribe of amazing women was created.

The authors in this book are your tribe. They want the best for you. That is the reason they took the time and energy to be a part of the book. Behind each chapter, the author's bio and contact information is included. Connect with them. The authors are excited to cheer you on!

~Jodi Brandstetter and Melanie Booher, Co-Founders, Influence Network Media

https://authors.influencenetworkmedia.com

About the Publisher:

Influence Network Media

We provide publishing & promotional services to business experts who want to become authors.

A media company that provides publishing and promotional coaching and services to authors who write non-fiction books around people in business. Founded by Jodi Brandstetter and Melanie Booher, Influence Network Media is a one-stop-shop to ensure your book is a bestseller and authors are able to use their book as a vessel to their career success.

Our offerings include:
- **Overnight Author** where in two days you are an author of one of our collective book series.
- **Collective Book** Opportunities where you only need one chapter, bio and headshot to become an Amazon Best Selling Author!
- **Solo Bundle** Opportunities for Business Experts who want to write a book that becomes a course and presentation all in one.
- **Micro Book** Opportunity for Business Experts that is less than 100 pages.

To learn more:
https://authors.influencenetworkmedia.com
Publishing@LETSCincy.com

Influence Network *Media*

Collaborative Book Series

Women in Business

A Book Series Dedicated to the future generations of Women Business Leaders

Book Smarts Business Podcast

Short on time but big on growth? Then the Book Smarts Business Podcast is the podcast for you – the experienced, business professional who loves to listen to podcasts and read business books all in an effort to learn more about his/her profession, become an expert in their field, or maybe even become an entrepreneur down the road!

In 15 minutes, you will learn more about the expert authors, gain amazing insights and knowledge from their unique expertise, as well as the ins & outs about their book, and why they decided to write their book!

For a potential author, Book Smarts Business Podcast provides an avenue for business authors to showcase their expertise and book, and gain more readers for their book!

https://booksmartsbusiness.buzzsprout.com/

www.ingramcontent.com/pod-product-compliance
Lightning Source LLC
Chambersburg PA
CBHW050007230526
45465CB00003BB/1294